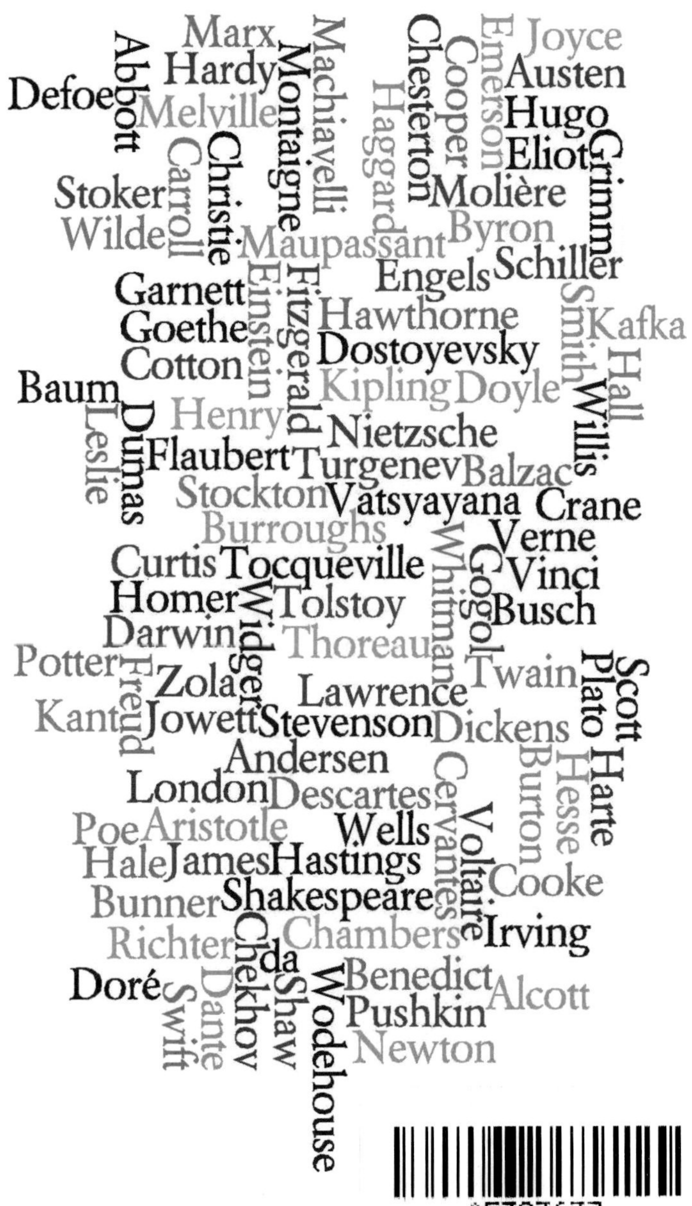

Defoe
Abbott
Marx
Hardy
Melville
Montaigne
Machiavelli
Haggard
Chesterton
Cooper
Emerson
Joyce
Austen
Hugo
Eliot
Grimm
Stoker
Carroll
Christie
Maupassant
Fitzgerald
Einstein
Engels
Byron
Schiller
Molière
Wilde
Garnett
Goethe
Cotton
Hawthorne
Dostoyevsky
Smith
Kafka
Hall
Willis
Baum
Henry
Kipling
Doyle
Leslie
Dumas
Flaubert
Turgenev
Balzac
Nietzsche
Stockton
Vatsyayana
Crane
Burroughs
Verne
Curtis
Tocqueville
Whitman
Gogol
Vinci
Homer
Widger
Tolstoy
Busch
Darwin
Thoreau
Potter
Freud
Twain
Scott
Plato
Harte
Kant
Zola
Jowett
Lawrence
Dickens
Burton
Hesse
Stevenson
Andersen
London
Descartes
Cervantes
Voltaire
Poe
Aristotle
Wells
Hale
James
Hastings
Cooke
Bunner
Shakespeare
Irving
Richter
Chambers
Doré
Dante
Swift
Chekhov
da
Shaw
Wodehouse
Benedict
Pushkin
Alcott
Newton
AF303637

tredition

tredition was established in 2006 by Sandra Latusseck and Soenke Schulz. Based in Hamburg, Germany, tredition offers publishing solutions to authors and publishing houses, combined with world-wide distribution of printed and digital book content. tredition is uniquely positioned to enable authors and publishing houses to create books on their own terms and without conventional manufacturing risks.

For more information please visit: www.tredition.com

TREDITION CLASSICS

This book is part of the TREDITION CLASSICS series. The creators of this series are united by passion for literature and driven by the intention of making all public domain books available in printed format again - worldwide. Most TREDITION CLASSICS titles have been out of print and off the bookstore shelves for decades. At tredition we believe that a great book never goes out of style and that its value is eternal. Several mostly non-profit literature projects provide content to tredition. To support their good work, tredition donates a portion of the proceeds from each sold copy. As a reader of a TREDITION CLASSICS book, you support our mission to save many of the amazing works of world literature from oblivion. See all available books at www.tredition.com.

Project Gutenberg

The content for this book has been graciously provided by Project Gutenberg. Project Gutenberg is a non-profit organization founded by Michael Hart in 1971 at the University of Illinois. The mission of Project Gutenberg is simple: To encourage the creation and distribution of eBooks. Project Gutenberg is the first and largest collection of public domain eBooks.

Humanity in the City

E. H. (Edwin Hubbell) Chapin

Imprint

This book is part of TREDITION CLASSICS

Author: E. H. (Edwin Hubbell) Chapin
Cover design: Buchgut, Berlin – Germany

Publisher: tredition GmbH, Hamburg - Germany
ISBN: 978-3-8472-1664-3

www.tredition.com
www.tredition.de

Copyright:
The content of this book is sourced from the public domain.

The intention of the TREDITION CLASSICS series is to make world literature in the public domain available in printed format. Literary enthusiasts and organizations, such as Project Gutenberg, world-wide have scanned and digitally edited the original texts. tredition has subsequently formatted and redesigned the content into a modern reading layout. Therefore, we cannot guarantee the exact reproduction of the original format of a particular historic edition. Please also note that no modifications have been made to the spelling, therefore it may differ from the orthography used today.

HUMANITY IN THE CITY.

E. H. Chapin
Engraved by J. C. Buttre

HUMANITY IN THE CITY.

BY THE
REV. E. H. CHAPIN.

NEW YORK:
DE WITT & DAVENPORT, PUBLISHERS,
160 & 162 NASSAU STREET.

BOSTON:
ABEL TOMPKINS, 38 & 40 CORNHILL.

G. W. ALEXANDER,
BINDER,
9 Spruce Street.
W. H. TINSON.
STEREOTYPER,
24 Beekman Street.
TAWS, RUSSELL & CO.
PRINTERS,
No. 26 Beekman Street.

PREFACE.

A volume like the present hardly requires the formality of a preface. It is the continuation of a series already published, and, like that, aims at applying the highest standard of Morality and Religion to the phases of every-day life. In order, however, that the view with which these discourses have been prepared may not be misconceived, I wish merely to say that I am far from supposing that these are the only themes to be preached, or that they constitute the highest class of practical subjects, and shall be sorry [x] if in any way they seem to imply a neglect of that interior and holy life which is the spring not only of right affections, but of clear perception and sturdy, every-day duty. I hope, on the contrary, that the very aspects of this busy city life — the very problems which start out of it — will tend to convince men of the necessity of this inward and regenerating principle. Nevertheless, I maintain that these topics have a place in the circle of the preacher's work, and he need entertain no fear of desecrating his pulpit by secular themes, who seeks to consecrate all things in any way involving the action and the welfare of men, by the spirit and aims of His Religion who, while he preached the Gospel, likewise fed the hungry, healed the sick, and touched the issues of every temporal want. I may have failed in the method, I trust I have not in the purpose.

E. H. C.

New York, May, 1854.

THE LESSONS OF THE STREET.

HUMANITY IN THE CITY.

DISCOURSE I.

THE LESSONS OF THE STREET.

> Wisdom crieth without; she uttereth her voice in the streets. —
> Proverbs, i. 20.

The great truths of religion may be communicated to the mind and the heart in two ways—by abstract treatment, and by illustration. It must be taken up in its absolute connection with God, and with our own souls. In solitary meditation, in self-examination, and in prayer, we shall learn the intrinsic claims which Faith and Duty have upon reason and conscience. But we cannot proceed far before we discover the necessity of some *symbol*, by which these abstract principles may be made distinct to [14] us. And, looking around for this purpose, we find that all the phases of existence are full of spiritual illustration—full of religious suggestion and argument. Thus our Saviour pronounced his great doctrines of Eternal Life, and of Personal Religion, and then turned to the world for a commentary. Under his teaching nature became an illuminated missal, lettered by the lilies of the field, and pencilled with hues that played through the leaves of Olivet. The wild birds, in their flight, bore upward the beautiful lesson of Providence, and the significance of the Kingdom of Heaven was contained in a mustard-seed. By no abstruse reasoning did he make his instructions so vivid to his disciples, and so fresh to ourselves. But he awoke the conviction of moral need, and repentance, and Divine Love, by drawing from instances with which they had been familiar all their lives—the procedures of government, the transactions of business, the labors of the husbandman, and the incidents of home. And the result is essentially the same, whether we start with the religious truth to find some illustration in the world [15] around us, or from some aspect of human life, or nature, extract a religious truth. Nor need this always be sharply obvious. It is only necessary that our point of view be sufficiently elevated to throw a spiritual light upon things, and to reveal their moral relations; for, often, our understandings are cleared, and our hearts made better, by the mere scope and tendency of such observations.

With this conviction, I called your attention, last winter, to some of the "Aspects of City Life," and with the same view, I wish now to address you, for a few Sunday evenings, on the Conditions of Humanity in the City, in which series I shall endeavor not only to present new topics of interest, but to urge more explicitly some points, which, in the afore-mentioned discourses, I merely touched upon.

The essential meaning of the personification in the text is in accordance, I think, with the general tenor of remark which I have just been making. For I understand it to mean, that everything is instructive, that even in the common ways of life the most important truths, and the profoundest moral and reli [16] gious significance, are contained. And the words before us, also, specifically indicate the subject upon which I wish to speak this evening, for they declare that "Wisdom... uttereth her voice in the streets."

The street through which you walk every day; with whose sights and sounds you have been familiar, perhaps, all your lives; is it all so common-place that it yields you no deep lessons,—deep and fresh, it may be, if you would only look around with discerning eyes? Engaged with your own special interests, and busy with monotonous details, you may not heed it; and yet there is something finer than the grandest poetry, even in the mere spectacle of these multitudinous billows of life, rolling down the long, broad, avenue. It is an inspiring lyric, this inexhaustible procession, in the misty perspective ever lost, ever renewed, sweeping onward between its architectural banks to the music of innumerable wheels; the rainbow colors, the silks, the velvets, the jewels, the tatters, the plumes, the faces—no two alike—shooting out from unknown depths, and passing away for ever—perpetually sweep [17] ing onward in the fresh air of morning, under the glare of noon, under the fading, flickering light, until the shadow climbs the tallest spire, and night comes with revelations and mysteries of its own.

And yet this changeful tide of activity is no mere lyric. It is an epic, rather, unfolding in its progress the contrasts, the conflicts, the heroisms, the failures, — in one word, the great and solemn issues of human life. And a few comprehensive lessons from that "Wisdom which uttereth her voice in the streets," may prove a fitting introduction, from which we can pass to consider more specific conditions of humanity in the city.

Taking up the subject in this light, I observe that the first lesson of the street is in the illustration which it affords us of the *diversities of human conditions*. The most superficial eye recognizes this. A city is, in one respect, like a high mountain; the latter is an epitome of the physical globe; for its sides are belted by products of every zone, from the tropical luxuriance that clusters around its base, to its arctic summit far up in the sky. So is the [18] city an epitome of the social world. All the belts of civilization intersect along its avenues. It contains the products of every moral zone. It is cosmopolitan, not only in a national, but in a spiritual, sense. Here you may find not only the finest Saxon culture, but the grossest barbaric degradation. There you pass a form of Caucasian development, the fine-cut features, the imperial forehead, the intelligent eye, the confident tread, the true port and stature of a man. But who is this that follows in his track; under the same national sky, surrounded by the same institutions, and yet with those pinched features, that stunted form, that villainous look; is it Papuan, Bushman, or Carib? Fitly representing either of these, though born in a Christian city, and bearing about not only the stamp of violated physical law, but of moral neglect and baseness. And no one needs to be told that there are savages in New York, as well as in the islands of the sea. Savages, not in gloomy forests, but under the strength of gas-light, and the eyes of policemen; with war-whoops and clubs very much the same, and garments as fantastic, and souls [19] as brutal, as any of their kindred at the antipodes. China, India, Africa, will you not find their features in some circles of the social world right around you? Idolatry! you cannot find any more gross, any more cruel, on the broad earth, than within the area of a mile around this pulpit. Dark minds from which God is obscured; deluded souls, whose fetish is the dice-box or the bottle; apathetic spirits, steeped in sensual abomination, unmoved by a moral ripple, soaking in the slump of animal vitality. False gods, more hideous, more awful, than Moloch or Baal; worshipped with shrieks, worshipped with curses, with the hearthstone for the bloody altar, and the drunken husband for the immolating priest, and women and children for the victims. I have no terms of respect too high for the brave and conscientious men who carry the gospel, and their own lives, in their hands to distant shores. But, surely, they need not go thus far to *seek* for the benighted and the debased. They may find there a wider extent of heathenism, but none more intense than that which prevails close by the school and the [20] church. The richest products of modern progress and Christian culture grow on the verge of barren wastes, and jungles of violence, and "the region of the shadow of death."

In the street, however, not only do we behold these different degrees of civilization, but those problems of diversity, which the highest form of existing civilization developes—the diversities of extreme poverty, and extreme wealth, for instance. Here sits the beggar, sick and pinched with cold; and there goes a man of no better flesh and blood, and no more authentic charter of soul, wrapped in comfort, and actually bloated with luxury. There issues the whine of distress, beside the glittering carriage-wheels. There, amidst the rush of gaiety; the busy, selfish whirl; half naked, shivering, with her bare feet on the icy pavement, stands the little girl, with the shadow of an experience upon her that has made her preternaturally old, and it may be, driven the angel from her face. Still, we cannot believe that above that wintry heaven which stretches over her, there is less regard for the poor, neglected child, than for that [21] rosy belt of infant happiness which girdles and gladdens ten thousand hearths.

And here, too, through the brilliant street, and the broad light of day, walks Purity, enshrined in the loveliest form of womanhood. And along that same street by night, attended by fitting shadows, strolls womanhood discrowned, clothed with painted shame, yet, even in the springs of that guilty heart not utterly quenched. We render just homage to the one, we pour scorn upon the other; but, could we trace back the lines of circumstance, and inquire why the one stands guarded with such sweet respect, and why the other has fallen, we might raise problems with which we cannot tax Providence, which we may not lay altogether to the charge of the condemned, but for which we might challenge an answer from society.

And, if we would ascertain the practical purport of this lesson of human diversity which is so conspicuous in the street — the meaning of these sharp contrasts of refinement and grossness, intelligence and ignorance, respectability and guilt — we only ask a question [22] that thousands have asked before us. And yet, it is possible to surmise the purpose of these diversities. We know, for one thing, that out of them come some of the noblest instances of character and of achievement. Ignorance and crime and poverty and vice, stand in fearful contrast to knowledge and integrity and wealth and purity; but they likewise constitute the dark background against which the virtues of human life stand out in radiant relief; virtues developed by the struggle which they create; virtues which seem impossible without their co-existence. For, whence issues any such thing as *virtue*, except out of the temptation and antagonism of vice? How could *Charity* ever have appeared in the world, were there no dark ways to be trodden by its bright feet, and no suffering and sadness to require its aid? I look at these asylums, these hospitals, these ragged schools — a zodiac of beautiful charities, girdling all this selfishness and sin — I look at these monuments which humanity will honor when war shall be but a legend, and laurels have withered to dust; and when I think what they have grown out of, [23] and why they stand here, I regard them as so many sublime way-marks by which Providence unfolds its purposes among men, and by which men trace out the plan of God.

And then, again, perhaps this problem of human diversity presses heaviest where civilization is the most advanced, in order that men may be more sharply aroused to seek some practical solution. It is an encouraging sign when an evil begins to be intensely felt, and the demand for relief becomes desperate. The civilization of our time is imperfect; involves many incongruities; perhaps creates some evils; but that it is an improved civilization, is evinced by the fact that it is *self-conscious*; for perception is the necessary antecedent of endeavor and success. The contrasts of human condition, then, that unfold themselves in the crowded street, may teach us our duty and our responsibility in lessening social inequality and need.

But a solution of this problem, clearer perhaps than any other, appears when we consider another lesson of the street; a lesson which requires us to look a little deeper, but which, [24] when we do look, is no less evident than these diversities. That lesson unfolds the essential *unity* of humanity. For, we find that the differences between men are *formal* rather than *real*; that, with various outward conditions, they pass through the same great trials; and that the scales which seem to hang uneven at the surface, and to be tipped this way and that by the currents of worldly fortune, are very nearly balanced in the depths of the inner life. We are shallow judges of the happiness or the misery of others, if we estimate it by any marks that distinguish them from ourselves; if, for instance, we say that because they have more money they are happier, or because they live more meagrely they are more wretched. For, men are allied by much more than they differ. The rich man, rolling by in his chariot, and the beggar, shivering in his rags, are allied by much more than they differ. It is safer, therefore, to estimate our neighbor's real condition by what we find in our own lot, than by what we do not find there. And now, see into what an essential unity this criterion draws the jostling, divergent masses [25] in yonder street! Each man there, like all the rest, finds life to be a discipline. Each has his separate form of discipline; but it bears upon the kindred spirit that is in every one of us, and strikes upon motives, sympathies, faculties, that run through the common humanity. Surely, you will not calculate any *essential* difference from mere appearances; for the light laughter that bubbles on the lip often mantles over brackish depths of sadness, and the serious look may be the sober veil that covers a divine peace. You know that the bosom *can* ache beneath diamond brooches, and how many blithe hearts dance under coarse wool. But I do not allude merely to these accidental contrasts. I mean that about equal measures of trial, equal measures of what men call good and evil, are allotted to all; enough, at least, to prove the identity of our humanity, and to show that we are all subjects of the same great plan. You say that the poor man who passes yonder, carrying his burden, has a hard lot of it, and it may be he has; but the rich man who brushes by him has a hard lot of it too—just as hard for *him*, just as well fitted to dis [26] cipline him for the great ends of life. He has his money to take care of; a pleasant occupation, you may think; but, after all, an *occupation*, with all the strain and anxiety of labor, making more hard work for him, day and night, perhaps, than his neighbor has who digs ditches or thumps a lapstone. And it is quite likely that he feels poorer than the poor man, and, if he ever becomes self-conscious, has great reason to feel meaner. And then, he has his rivalries, his competitions, his troubles of caste and etiquette, so that the merchant, in his sumptuous apartments, comes to the same essential point, "sweats, and bears fardels," as well as his brother in the garret; tosses on his bed with surfeit, or perplexity, while the other is wrapped in peaceful slumber; and, if he is one who recognizes the moral ends of life, finds himself called upon to contend with his own heart, and to fight with peculiar temptations. And thus the rich man and the poor man, who seem so unequal in the street, would find but a thin partition between them, could they, as they might, detect one another kneeling on the same platform of spiritual endeavor, and [27] sending up the same prayers to the same eternal throne.

But, say you, "here is one who is returning to a home of destitution, of misery; where the light of the natural day is almost shut out, but in which brood the deeper shadows of despair." And yet, in many a splendid mansion you will find a more fearful destitution, a dearth of affections, killed by envy, jealousy, distrust; stifled by glittering formalities; a brood of evil passions that mock the splendor, and darken the magnificent walls. The measure of joy, too, is distributed with the same impartiality as the measure of woe. The child's grief throbs against the round of its little heart as heavily as the man's sorrow; and the one finds as much delight in his kite or drum, as the other in striking the springs of enterprise or soaring on the wings of fame. After all, happiness is the rule, not the exception, even in the hearts that beat in the crowded city; and its great elements are as common as the air, and the sunshine, and free movement, and good health. And what the fortunate may seem to gain in variety of methods, may only [28] be unconscious devices to simulate or recover that natural relish which others have never lost. And no one doubts that the great dispensations of life, the events that make epochs in our fleeting years, cleave through all the strata of outward difference, and lay bare the core of our one humanity. Sickness! does it not make Dives look very much like Lazarus, and show our common weakness, and reveal the common marvel of this "harp of thousand strings?" And sorrow! it veils all faces, and bows all forms alike, and sends the same shudder through the frame, and casts the same darkness upon the walls, and peals forth in the same dirge of maternal agony by the dead boy's cradle in the sumptuous chamber, and the baby's last sleep on its bed of straw. And Death! how wonderfully it makes them all alike who in the street wore such various garments, and had such distinct aims, and were whirled apart in such different orbits! Ah! our essential humanity comes out in those composed forms and still features. Those divergent currents have carried them out upon the same placid sea at last; and the same [29] solemn light streams upon the clasped hands and the uplifted faces. We don't mind the drapery so much then. It seems a very superficial matter beside the silent and starless mystery that enfolds them all.

In what I have thus said I do not mean to maintain that outward conditions are nothing. I think they are a great deal; and we do right in striving to improve them; in escaping the evil, and seeking to secure the good that pertains to them. But, I repeat, when we come to the essential humanity, to the real discipline and substance of life, we find the same great features; and so this lesson of the street may help explain the problem suggested by the other; may reconcile each of us to our condition in the crowd, and direct our attention to substantial results.

But, again, the street, with its processions and activities, teaches us that much in human life is merely *phenomenal*, merely *appears*. We enter into this truth by a very common train of observation. We know how much is put on purposely for the public gaze, and has no other intention than to be seen; how hollow [30] are many of the smiles, and gay looks, and smooth decencies. And even the complexion of some, with its red and white, is more unsubstantial than all the rest; for it is in danger of being washed away by the first shower. It is strange to meet people whose personal significance in life is that of a shop window exhibiting lace and jewelry; strange to encounter men in whose place we might substitute a well-dressed effigy, and they would hardly be missed. Of course appearances should be attended to, and are good in their place. It is right that we should honor society by our best looks and ways. But it is not merely ridiculous, it is sad, to think how much in the street, where humanity exhibits all its phases, is appearance and but little else.

But dress and manners are not all that is phenomenal in human life. These men and women themselves, this streaming crowd, these brick walls and stately pinnacles, those that pursue and the things that are pursued, are only appearances. It may be profitable for us to stand apart from this multitude, this river of living forms, and think in how short a time it all [31] will have passed away; how short a time since, and it was not! A little while ago, and this rich and populous city was a green island, and our beautiful bay clasped it in its silver arms like an emerald. The wilderness stood here, and the child of the forest thought of it as a prepared abiding place for himself and for his people for ever. The red man has gone; the wild woods have vanished; and these structures, and vehicles, and busy crowds, have come into their places magically, like the new picture in a dissolving view. But are these forms of life, is your presence here or mine, any more substantial than those that have sunk away? Nay, all this splendid civilization, what is it but a sparkling ripple in the calm eternity of God? Dwellings, stores, banks, churches, streets, and the restless multitudes, are but forms of life,—as it were a rack of cloud drifting across the mirror of absolute being. That which seems to you substantial is only spectral. And as the dress of the fop, and the smile of the coquette, is merely an appearance; so the wealth for which men strain in eager chase, and the [32] fabrics which pride builds up, the anvils on which labor strikes its mighty blows, and the body to which so much is devoted, and which absorbs so much care, are but appearances also. While that which may seem to you as a shadow—the spiritual substratum of life, the basis of those spiritual laws which run through all our conditions—is the only abiding substance.

If we only look in this light, my friends, upon the continuous spectacle of human movement and human change, we shall find that "Wisdom... uttereth her voice in the streets." Old as the thought may be, in the rush of the great crowd it will come to us fresh and impressively, that all this is but a form of spiritual and eternal being. A day in the city is like life itself. Out of unconscious slumber into the brilliant morning and the thick activity we come. But, by-and-by, the heaving mass breaks into units, and one by one dissolves into the shadow of the night. Two cities grow up side by side—the city in which men appear, the city into which they vanish;

the city whose houses and goods they possess for a little while [33] and then leave behind them, and the city whose white monuments just show us the pinnacles of their estates in the eternal world. The busy, diversified crowd that rolls through the streets—it is only an appearance! It is a ceaseless march of emigration. In a little while, the names in this year's Directory may be read in Greenwood.

But we must not rest with this as the final lesson of the street. It is only the form of Life that is transient and phenomenal; but the *Life* itself is here, also—here, in these flashing eyes, and heaving breasts, and active limbs. These conditions, however transient, involve the great interest of Humanity; and that lends the deepest significance to these conditions. The interest of Humanity! which gives importance to all it touches, and transforms nature into history; which imparts dignity to the rudest workshop, and the most barren shore, and the humblest grave—this permits us to draw no mean or discouraging conclusions from the achievements and the changes of the multitudes around us. It may do for the skeptic, who sees nothing in existence but these [34] forms of things; who sees nothing but the limited phenomena of our present state, and thinks that includes all; it may do for him to croak over the transitoriness of life, and call it a trivial game. But it is *not* trivial; and there is no spot where man acts, there is nothing that he does, that is insignificant. Perhaps you have a quick eye for the foibles of people, and can detect their vanities, and meannesses, and laughable conceits. If you employ this gift to correct a bad habit, or expose a falsehood, it is well enough. But if it induces you to look upon things merely with the skill of a satirist, then let me say, there is no "ludicrous side" to life; there is nothing in human conduct that is simply absurd. The least transaction has a moral cast, and every word and act reveals spiritual relations. The interest of man can never be thrown into insignificance by his conditions; these draw interest from him. And, whatever his post in the world, however limited or broad his sphere of observation, for *him* life is real, and has intense relations. We must not stand so far apart from the crowd as to occupy the position of mere spectators, [35] and regard these men and women as so many mechanical figures in a panorama. We must look through the depths of their experience into their own souls, and through the depths of that experience again upon the world, beholding it as it appears to the beggar, and the lonely woman, and the child of vice and crime, and the hero, and the saint, and as it falls with intense yet diverse refractions upon all these multiform angles of personality. So shall we learn to cherish a solemn and tender interest in the dear humanity around us, and feel the arteries of sympathy which connect it, in all its conditions, with our own hearts. And, as we return homeward from our study of the street, it may be with our irritation, and prejudice, and selfishness softened down; with a larger love flowing out towards the least, and even the worst; realizing the spiritual ties that make us one, and the Infinite Fatherhood that encircles us all; perhaps suggestions will come to us that have been best expressed in the words of the poet—

> "Let us move slowly through the street,
> Filled with an ever-shifting train,
> [36] Amid the sound of steps that beat
> The murmuring walks like autumn rain.

> "How fast the flitting figures come!
> The mild, the fierce, the stony face;
> Some bright with thoughtless smiles, and some
> Where secret tears have left their trace.

> * * * * * * *

> "Each, where his tasks or pleasures call
> They pass, and heed each other not.
> There is, Who heeds, Who holds them all,
> In His large love and boundless thought.

> "These struggling tides of life that seem,
> In wayward, aimless course to tend,
> Are eddies of the mighty stream
> That rolls to its appointed end."

[37]

MAN AND MACHINERY.

[38]

[39]

DISCOURSE II.

MAN AND MACHINERY.

For the spirit of the living creature was in the wheels. — Ezekiel, i.
20.

Whatever may have been the significance of the sublime vision from which I have extracted those words, I do not think that their essential meaning is perverted when I apply them to the subject which comes before us this evening. I am not aware of any sentence that expresses more concisely the relation which I would indicate between *Man* and *Machinery*; between those great agents of human achievement and the living intelligence which works in them and by them. And though a Divine Spirit moved in those flashing splendors which burned before the eyes of the prophet, is it not also a divine spirit that mingles in every great manifestation of human [40] ity, and that moves even in the action of man, the worker, toiling among innumerable wheels?

Perhaps if we were called upon to name some one feature of the present age which distinguishes it from all other ages, and endows it with a special wonder and glory, we should call it the Age of Machinery. We trust our age is unfolding something better than material triumphs. The results of past thought and past endeavor are pouring through it in expanding currents of knowledge, liberty, and brotherhood. But the great *agents* in this diffusion of ideas and principles are those vehicles of iron, and those messengers of lightning, which compress the huge globe into a neighborhood, and bring all its interests within the system of a daily newspaper. Like the generations which have preceded us, we enter into the labors of others, and inherit the fruits of their effort. But these powerful instruments, condensing time and space, endow a single half-century with the possibilities of a cycle. If we take the period comprehending the American and the French revolutions as a dividing line, and look both sides the chasm, [41] we shall discover the difference of a thousand years. Remarkable for brilliant achievements in every department of physics, ours well deserves to be called the Age of *Science,* also. But it is still more remarkable, for the application of the most majestic and subtle constituents of the universe to the most familiar uses; the wild forces of matter have been caught and harnessed. Go into any factory, and see what fine workmen we have made of the great elements around us. See how magnificent nature has humbled itself, and works in shirt-sleeves. Without food, without sweat, without weariness, it toils all day at the loom, and shouts lustily in the sounding wheels. How diligently the iron fingers pick and sort, and the muscles of steel retain their faithful gripe, and enormous energies run to and fro with an obedient click; while forces that tear the arteries of the earth and heave volcanoes, spin the fabric of an infant's robe, and weave the flowers in a lady's brocade.

I think, then, we may appropriately call it—The Age of Machinery. It is not a peculiarity of the city, but, rather, seeks room to [42] stretch itself out; and so you may perceive its smoky signals hovering over a thousand vallies, and the echo of its mighty pulses throbbing among the loneliest hills. Nevertheless, it is sufficiently developed here to illustrate the Conditions of Humanity in the City, and this fact, together with the general interest of the subject, is my warrant for taking it up in the present discourse. And my remarks must necessarily be of a general cast, as I have no room for the statistics, and details, and various discussions which grow out of the theme.

And the key-note of all that I shall say, at the present time, is really in the text itself—"For the spirit of the living creature was in the wheels."

In the first place, these words suggest the relations of *Use* and *Help* between Man and Machinery. Upon surveying these numerous and complicated instruments, the thought that most readily occurs, perhaps, is that of the *necessity* of machinery. The very first step that man takes, out of the condition of infant weakness and animal rudeness, must be accomplished by the aid of some implement. He [43] alone, of all beings upon the face of the earth, is obliged to *invent*, and is capable of endless invention. The necessity for this springs out, and is a prophecy of, his destiny. The moment he was seen fashioning the first tool, however imperfect, that moment was indicated the difference between himself and the brute, and the control he was destined to gain over the world about him. To fulfil this destiny, he confronts nature with naked hands; and yet, there is the earth to plough, the harvest to reap, the torrent to bridge, the ocean to cross; there are all the results to achieve which constitute the difference between the primitive man, and the civilization of the nineteenth century. The Machine, then—the agent which links the gratification to the want—is born of necessity. But we must make a distinction between those instruments which are positively essential, and those, for instance, which merely answer the demands of luxury or indolence.

And this brings up the question of the *comparative* uses of Machinery—the foremost place being assigned to those implements which are absolutely indispensable to man's existence [44] upon the earth. But between this absolute degree, and that of frivolous invention, there are countless grades of utility. And the question of usefulness must be decided according to the *standard* of utility which we apply. If bare subsistence is assumed to be the end of man upon the earth, most of our modern inventions are useless. We can travel without a locomotive, and procure a meal without a cooking-range. The moment we rise above the grossest conception of human existence, the test of usefulness becomes enlarged, and we can make a safe decision upon whatever increases man's comfort, adds to his ability, or inspires his culture. In this way, new things *become* indispensable. That which was not necessary *à priori, is* necessary now, in a fresh stage of development, and in connection with circumstances that have sprung up and formed around it. That which was not necessary to man the savage, living on roots and raw fish, is necessary to man the civilized, with new possibilities opening before him, and new faculties unfolded within him. The printing-press was not absolutely necessary to Nimrod, or to [45] Julius Cæsar, but is it not absolutely necessary now? Strike it out of existence to-day, and what would be the condition of the world to-morrow? You would have to tear away with it all that has grown up around it, and become assimilated to it—the textures of the world's growth for three hundred years. Paul moved the old world without a telegraph, and Columbus found a new one without a steamship. But see how essential these agents are to the present condition of civilization. How many derangements among the wheels of business, and the plans of affection, if merely a snow-drift blocks the cars, or a thunder-storm snaps the wires! Our estimate of necessity, and, therefore, of utility, must be formed according to present conditions, and the legitimate demand that rises out of them; these conditions themselves being the necessary developments of society and of the individual.

But some of these, you may say, are the demands of luxury, of indolent ease, of man setting nature to work and lapsing in self-indulgence. To some degree this result may grow out of the present state of things; as [46] some portion of evil will follow in the sweep of an immense good. But what is the precise sentence to be passed upon this prevalent luxury? Of course, admitting the evil — which is apparent — I maintain that there is a great deal of good in it; that it is inextricably associated with much real refinement and progress. Men are accustomed to speak of the simplicity and purity of past times, and to compare, with a sigh, the good old era of the stage-coach and the spinning-wheel with these days of whizzing machinery, Aladdin palaces, and California gold. But the core of logic that lies within this rind of sentiment forces a conclusion that I can by no means admit, the conclusion that the world is going backward. I never knew of an epoch that was not thought by some then living to be the worst that ever was, and which did not seem to stand in humiliating contrast with some blessed period gone by. But the golden age of Christianity is in the future, not in the past. Those old ages are like the landscape that shows best in purple distance, all verdant and smooth and bathed in mellow light. But could we go back and touch the reality, we [47] should find many a swamp of disease, and rough and grimy paths of rock and mire. Those were good old times, it may be thought, when baron and peasant feasted together. But the one could not read, and made his mark with a sword-pommel; and the other was not held so dear as a favorite dog. Pure and simple times were those of our grandfathers, — it may be. Possibly not so pure as we may think, however, and with a simplicity ingrained with some bigotry and a good deal of conceit. The fact is, we are bad enough, imperfect, not because we are growing worse, but because we are yet far from the best. I think, however, with Lord Bacon, that *these* are "the old times." The world is older now than it ever was, and it contains the best life and fruition of the past. And this special condition of luxury is a growth out of the past, and is the necessary concomitant of much that is good. Opening new channels for industry, it furnishes occupation for thousands; while, in many of its phases, it indicates a refined culture, and a sphere elevated above the imperative wants of existence. It is no proof of the disadvantages [48] of machinery, therefore, to say that it ministers to something beside absolute bodily need, and delivers man from a slow and exhausting drudgery. So far as it helps us to control nature, and increases the facilities of human intercourse, and diffuses general comfort and elegance, and affords a respite from incessant physical toil, so far it is an agent and a sign of progress.

But, it may be said again, that it is the agent of a selfish and exclusive power, enriching a few and injuring many. And it cannot be denied that grave problems grow out of the relations between Machinery and the laboring classes. Every little while, some new invention is thrust forward, which takes a portion of labor out of the hands of flesh and transfers it to hands of iron. It is not enough to say that mankind in general is benefited by these inanimate agents, which do the work of the world so much more rapidly and powerfully. This may answer as an argument against a monopoly of any one kind of mechanical force. It may be a reason for using cars instead of steamboats, and balloons rather than railroads. [49] The general good must be advanced, whatever the damage to private interests. But the present case brings up the question whether machinery is a general good at all; whether the effect of its introduction into almost every department of labor, will not be felt in the destitution of millions. And, upon this point, I observe, that, like all other great revolutions, the immediate effect may be such as has been suggested. But the final result will be beneficial, and such a result may be traced out even now. For instance, this clogging of old departments of labor will precipitate men upon fresh ones, and upon those that have been too much neglected. It will tend to introduce woman to branches of industry perfectly suited to her, but which have been too exclusively occupied by the other sex, and to turn the attention of robust men to those great fields of productive toil which are as yet but little improved. It may drive them from the dependence, the crowded competition, the unwholesome life of the city, into the broad fields and open air and the sovereignty of the soil. And if this immense intrusion of machinery has [50] only this result, of equalizing the balance against production, we shall have one solution of the problem. And there will be another solution, if this phalanx of mechanism shall lift the mass of men above the occasions of coarse material drudgery into other activities, which doubt-less will be thrown open, and shall allow more leisure for spiritual culture. But in this, and all other great questions affecting human welfare, I throw myself back, finally, upon the tokens of Providential Design. The world moves forward, not backward; and the great developments of time are for good, not evil. By machinery, man proceeds with his dominion over nature. He assimilates it to himself; it becomes, so to speak, a part of himself. Every great invention is the enlargement of his own personality. Iron and fire become blood and muscle, and gravitation flows in the current of his will. His pulses beat in the steamship, throbbing through the deep, while the fibres of his heart and brain inclose the earth in an electric network of thought and sympathy. That which was given to help man, will not hinder nor hurt [51] him. "For the spirit of the living creature is in the wheels."

I observe, in the second place, that the words of the text accord with the testimony which machinery bears to the *dignity of man*. All these great inventions — these implements of marvellous skill and power — prove that the inventor, or the worker, himself is *not* a machine. I know of nothing which gives me so forcible an impression of the worth and superiority of mind, of its alliance with the Creative Intelligence, as the exhibition of an ingenious piece of mechanism. I have stood with wonder before such a specimen, and seen it work with all the precision of a reflecting creature. Lifting the most tremendous weights, cleaving the most solid masses, performing the nicest tasks, as though a living intellect were in it, informing it and directing its power. I hardly know of any achievement that stands as a higher witness for the human mind. The great poem that bursts in a flood of inspiration upon the soul of genius, and opens the realms of immortal beauty, may lift us to a nobler plane of endeavor. The heroic act of toil or [52] martyrdom for principle, certainly has a loftier, because it is a moral, grandeur. But as an illustration of the *creativeness* of man's intellect — of its wondrous capability — of its alliance with that attribute of the Divine Nature which is evident in the fibres of the grass-blade and the march of the galaxy — I know of nothing more striking than this piece of mechanism, which is the product of the most profound and patient thought, the harmonizing of antagonistic forces, the combination of the most abstruse details, fitted to the remotest exigencies, and working just as the inventive mind meant it should, and just as it was set a-going, as if that mind were presiding over it, were in it, though it is now far distant, or has vanished from the earth. That mind is immortal! that nature, which is common to all men, transcends any shape of matter and is superior to mechanism. And it may be necessary to say this, necessary to say that man, who is helped by machinery, is *separate* from it. It is mind that is thus involved with matter. The spirit of a living creature that is in the wheels.

[53]

It may be necessary to say this, my friends, and to say it frequently, lest the vast mechanical achievements of our time seduce us into a mere mechanical life. I do not think that the deepest question is, whether machinery will multiply to such an extent as to snatch the bread from the mouths of living men; but whether men, with all the possibilities of their nature, will not become absorbed in that which supplies them with bread alone? I have just expressed my admiration for the genius of the great inventor. Nor can I honor too highly the faithful and industrious mechanic—the man who fills up his chink in the great economy by patiently using his hammer or his wheel. For, he *does* something. If he only sews a welt, or planes a knot, he helps build up the solid pyramid of this world's welfare. While there are those who, exhibiting but little use while living, might, if embalmed, serve the same purpose as those forms of ape and ibis *inside* the Egyptian caverns—serve to illustrate the shapes and idolatries of human conceit. At any rate, there is no doubt of the essential nobility of that man who pours into life the [54] honest vigor of his toil, over those who compose this feathery foam of fashion that sweeps along Broadway; who consider the insignia of honor to consist in wealth and indolence; and who, ignoring the family history, paint coats of arms to cover up the leather aprons of their grandfathers.

I shall not be misunderstood then, when, making a distinction in behalf of the mechanic by profession, I say that no man should be a mere mechanic in *soul*. In other words, no man should be bound up in a routine of material ends and uses. He should not be a mechanic, working exclusively in a dead system, but always the architect of a living ideal. And surrounded, astonished, served and enriched as we are by these splendid legions of mechanism, the danger is that material achievement will seem to us the *supreme* achievement; that all life will become machinery; and the higher interests of being, and the great firmament of immortality, be eclipsed by these flashing wheels. We are in danger of being drawn away from the sanctities of the inner life and the still work of the [55] soul, by this maelstrom of excitement and power. No religious man can help asking, and asking anxiously, whether the spirit of devotion is as deep and fresh, whether spiritual communion with God is as direct and constant, in this whirl and roar, and marvellous achievement, as they were in times bearing less evidently the signs of material progress. For, that which merely gives us a stronger grasp of the world around us, and sends us along the level of nature, is not the most genuine element of progress; but that which elevates our moral plane and enriches the great deep of our spiritual being. The steamship and telegraph are not absolute tokens of this progress, but the moral earnestness and the Christian charity that work through them are; and these must spring up in hearts that are not merely adjusted to the world, but lifted above it—that are not so occupied by mere machinery as to neglect the living streams of an inward and devout culture.

But, for another reason,—or as an extension of the same reason,—we need to realize the truth that man is separate from and superior [56] to machinery. It is because, upon a practical recognition of this truth depends the just action of all who control the interests of labor, and, so to speak, the lives and souls of the laborers. If we should beware of an influence that would render us *mere* mechanics in our own higher nature, we should likewise remove anything that makes others mere machines, presenting for us no other consideration than the amount of work they can perform for us, and with how little care and cost. I cannot now enter into the great questions that spring up here concerning the relations of capital and labor, and of the employer and the employed. I only observe that these are among the deepest questions of the time: questions which will be heard, which must be discussed, and practically answered. And they who by plans and experiments, however visionary they may seem, however abortive they may prove, are trying to solve this problem, are much wiser in their generation than those who content themselves with cutaneous palliatives and a stolid conservatism. But I maintain now, that back of all these considerations [57] stands this truism,—that man is not a machine; that the being who toils in the factory, the furnace, the dark mine underground, is one who needs and hopes and suffers and dies, as sinews of iron and fabrics of brass cannot. "The spirit of a living creature is in the wheels." A cry for justice, for free action, for spiritual opportunity, comes not from the roaring engine or the dizzy loom, but out from the midst of those who are endowed with the sensitiveness and the moral possibilities that belong to humanity, and humanity alone. Set in motion the grandest piece of mechanism ever conceived by human genius, and still there is infinite difference between it and the poorest drudge that bears God's image,—between it and any human claim.

It must have been a noble spectacle, a few weeks since, to have seen that great ship [A] sail out of port, stretching its proud beak over the sea, and with thundering exultation trampling its sapphire floor. One might have followed its wake with a glistening eye, and said [58] to himself—"There is the great symbol of human progress, there is the consummation of man's triumph over nature! The long results of ages are condensed in that fabric of strength and beauty. Man has compelled the forest, and ravished the mine, and converted the stream, and chained the fire; and now, with the eye of science and the hand of skill, he rides in this triumphal chariot, making a swift, obedient pathway of the deep!" But when that dark day burst upon them, and nature with one angry sweep transformed that splendid palace into a floating death-chamber; when ocean lifted up this triumph of man's skill, and shook it like a toy; the interest which hung over that awful desolation—the interest to which your hearts flow out with painful sympathy to-night—was in nothing that man had achieved, but in humanity itself. All the workmanship, all the material splendor, all the skill, were nothing compared with one heart beating amidst that tempest; compared with one groan that rose from that sea of agony, and then was silent for ever.

[Note A: This discourse was delivered just after the tidings of the loss of the San Francisco, in December, 1853.]

[59]

And, again, when I consider the conduct of that gallant captain who, day by day, rode by the side of the shuddering wreck, and in slippery peril maintained the royalty of his manhood, and sent a brother's cheer and a brother's help through the storm; when I think of that noble achievement where the Stars and Stripes and the Cross of St. George were lost and blended in the light of universal humanity; I say to myself—how does an act like this shed light upon a thousand instances of human depravity! What is any material triumph compared to this moral beauty! And what is the great distinction between rags and coronets, between senates and workshops, when in the breast of every man, and everywhere, there is the possibility of such heroism, such charity, and such splendid performance!

And so, my friends, turning from this specific illustration, and looking through the wards of cities, the busy factories, the dim attics and cellars, they all become glorious by the reflected light of the humanity that toils and suffers within them. Man is greater than any [60] achievement of mechanism, any interest of capital, and all the questions which these involve must be brought to the test of his moral capabilities, and his spiritual as well as earthly wants.

But I observe, finally, that the words of the text suggest the *Providential design* and the *Divine agency* that are involved in the great mechanical achievements of our age. As the Divine Spirit flowed through those living creatures and moved those wheels, so God's influence is in the movement of humanity, and in the instruments of that movement. We get only a narrow, and often an inexplicable conception of things, until we behold them encircled by this horizon of a Providential design. And if humanity, with all its claims and possibilities, is involved in this network of mechanism, so doubtless are the processes of Infinite Wisdom. Something more than material greatness, or ends limited merely to this earth, is to be wrought out by it. Indications of this appear already. The telegraph and steamship, for instance, serve not only the interests of trade and commerce, but of lib [61] erty, and brotherhood, and of Christian influence.

It is beautiful to see how the most selfish agents presently become converted to the broadest uses, and matter is transformed into the vehicle of spirit. For God is in history. It is a Divine dispensation, and has miracles of its own. And, because they come by natural development let us not fail to recognize the benevolence and the significance involved with them. Is not the effect of miracle in the electric wire? The printing-press, is it not the gift of tongues? It is atheistic to suppose that all these wondrous agents have only a narrow and material purpose, and play no part in the highest scheme of the world. Like the prophet by the river Chebar, we may behold them as the symbols in a sublime vision. These wheels within wheels, full of eyes, full of intelligence, and full of human destiny and vast purpose, we know not all their meaning yet. But they have a great meaning. Beneficent intention runs through their swift motions—voices of promise rise in their multitudinous sounds. A living spirit is in these wheels— [62] the influence of God; the spirit of man. And, in due time, out of them will evolve the incalculable issues of human welfare and the Divine glory.

[63]

THE STRIFE FOR PRECEDENCE.

[64]

[65]

DISCOURSE III.

THE STRIFE FOR PRECEDENCE.

And if a man strive for masteries, yet is he not crowned except he strive lawfully.—II. Timothy, ii. 5.

In walking the streets of the city, there rises the interesting question—What are the various motives which animate these restless people, and send them to and fro? As a French author has well observed,—"The necessaries of life do not occasion, at most, a third part of the hurry." They are comparatively few who struggle among these busy waves for a bare subsistence. There are others who are impelled by some of the deepest affections of the human heart, and who toil day after day with noble self-sacrifice for the comfort of dependent parents, and helpless children. While others still run on errands of mercy, and work in the harness of unrelaxing duty. But when we have [66] taken all these influences into the account, and made the most of them, there remains a large quantity of activity which, as we trace it to its spring, we shall find issuing from a desire for influence, for notoriety, for some kind of personal distinction. The city,—in this instance, as in many others, representing the world at large,—is essentially a race-course, or battle-field, in which, through forms of ambitious effort, and cunning method, and plodding labor, and ostentation, the aspirations of thousands appear and carry on a *Strife for Precedence.*

And, in selecting this phase of human life as the theme of the present discourse, I observe in the first place—that the desire for precedence is one of the *deepest* and most *subtle* motives in the soul of man. It is prolific of disguises. It is not merely under the mask which we may put on before other people, but it glides through various transformations of self-deceit; like the evil genius in the fairy tale, now dwindling to a mere seed, now bursting into a devouring fire. When, with an honest purpose, we probe it and pluck at it, [67] still we may detect it in the lowest socket of the heart. Often it is most vital when we feel most sure that it is vanquished. It delights in the garb of humility, and finds its food in the profession of self-renunciation. See its grossest expression in the desire for physical superiority—the glory of the victor in the Grecian games,

or the modern pugilist with the champion's belt. This is the reason
why men, priding themselves upon qualities in which they are
equalled by any mastiff and excelled by any horse, will stand up
and batter one another into a mass of blood and bruises. And if we
analyze the merit of some conqueror upon a hundred battle-fields,
we shall find ingredients almost as coarse. Only there was a larger
impulse, and more genius to light the way; so that *his* combat in the
ring became *achievement*, and his success *fame*. The outside difference was in the value of the stakes; but the huzzas did not rise much
nearer to heaven in the one instance than in the other. And when we
get at the real centre of all those plaudits, we find only a little throbbing atom, a little human [68] heart, all on fire with the lust for supremacy.

But these are the more palpable shapes of this desire for Precedence. It works more covertly, but with no less energy. I need not—
for I cannot—specify all the instances in which it acts. It would constitute a more concise statement to affirm where it does *not* act. It is
sufficiently apparent in the scramble of the market and the parade
of the street; at the toilette of beauty; in the etiquette of the drawing-
room, where people sit as if in a cavern of icicles; in the spurious
patriotism of politics; and too often, it is to be feared, in the highest
seats of the synagogue, and where men lift holy hands of prayer. It
is the scholar's inspiration. When he comes to the steep and rugged
way, it helps him to make a foot-hold, and the thorns blossom into
roses as he climbs. Sometimes, even, it saturates the plan of the
philanthropist, and peppers the milk of his charity with an inconsistent wrath.

It seems an unhappy, as it must often be an unjust method, to attribute any appearance of good conduct to the meanest possible
motive. [69] It is a policy that makes a man afraid of his best friends.
He feels that every draft he makes upon human honor, or affection,
is liable to be cashed with counterfeit bills. If there were no alternative between the cleverness that suspects everybody, and the credu-
lity that trusts everybody, I think I had rather be one of the dupes
than one of the oracles. For, really, there is less misery in being
cheated than in that kind of wisdom which perceives, or thinks it
perceives, that all mankind are cheats. But, while simple fact forbids
our assuming either of these extremes, we must, nevertheless, in

reasoning upon the phenomena of human conduct, allow large scope for the influence of which I am now treating. For, as I have already intimated, we shall find it lurking under numerous forms. In discussing the question of Slavery, for instance, it is often said — that it is for the interest of the master to take good care of his human as he does of his brute stock — to see that they are well-fed, clothed, &c. And so it is for his *interest* to do this. But how often does the lust for supremacy over-ride interest itself! [70] How often does an imperious personality thrust itself forward in the most absurd ways, damaging its own property and welfare, just as a boy breaks his top, or a balked rider shoots his horse, or an independent congregationalist locks his pew-door, as much as to say — "There, the world knows one thing about me, at least. It knows that I am *master* and *owner* here!"

But I observe, further, that, while this desire for Precedence is common among men of all conditions, there are some modes of its expression which are peculiarly excited in a democratic form of society. That which is the open glory of a community like ours, is with many a secret vexation and shame. People boast here of the equality of our institutions, and then try their best to break up the social level. In a genuine Aristocracy, where they have endeavored to preserve a gulf-stream of noble blood in the midst of the plebeian Atlantic, and a man holds his distinction by the color of the bark on his family tree, and the kind of sap that circulates through it, there is no danger of any unpleasant mistakes. The hard palm of Labor may cross the gloved hand [71] of Leisure, and nobody will suspect that the select is too familiar with the vulgar. Consequently, there is a good deal of affability and prime manliness, besides those associations of sentiment and imagination which, if there must be an aristocracy, lend it an artistic consistency. But here, where everybody says that all men are equal, and everybody is afraid they *will* be; where there are no adamantine barriers of birth and caste; people are anxiously exclusive. And though the forms of aristocracy flourish more gorgeously in their native soil, the genuine *virus* can be found in New York almost as readily as in London, or Vienna. And the virus breaks out in the most absurd shapes of liveries and titles. And these forms of aspiration are not only absurd because they are inconsistent, but because they illustrate no real ground of precedence. They are superficial and uncertain. They do not pertain to the man but to his accidents. He gains by them no intrinsic glory, no permanent good. To employ the language of the text, by these he strives for masteries; but he does not strive lawfully, and so he is not crowned. And this [72] leads me to say something respecting what is false, and what is legitimate, in that strife for Precedence which is so amply illustrated in the life of the City.

Let us, then, consider some of the forms which this struggle assumes in the streets and the dwellings around us. I remark, in the first place, that it inspires much of the effort for *wealth*. I believe there are but few, comparatively, who are anxious to make money merely for the sake of piling it up, and counting it out. There may be a mania of this kind, in which men become enamored of Mammon for his own sake, and hug him to their breasts, and kiss his golden lips, with all the ardor of lovers. Still, I suspect that the genuine miser — that is, one who loves money for itself alone — is an exceptional man. But every man who is not absolutely inactive and useless in the world, is moved by some kind of passion. For, it is not correct to speak of *outliving* our passions. We may outlive the passion of young, fresh love, that makes the world a May-time of blossoms and of roses. We may outlive the passion for selfish fame, [73] because some transcendent claim of duty snatches us up to a sublimer level. We may change these earlier forms for the passion of philanthropy, the passion for truth, the passion of holy conviction. But so long as we live at all, we do not outlive passion. And with many the most persistent desire is for that precedence which attends the possession of wealth. That miser, as you call him, with a face like parchment, and in whose nature all the springs of emotion seem to have grown rusty with long disuse, is animated by a secret flame that keeps him all a-glow. It is the consciousness of power — the mightiest power of the present age — the power of money. Those figures which he scrawls at his writing-desk involve a more potent magic than the cabalistic cyphers of Doctor Dee, or Cornelius Agrippa. His hand presses the spring of an influence that casts midnight or sunshine over the World of Traffic, and shakes entire blocks of real estate with a speculative earthquake. It is not the Czar or the Sultan, but the Capitalist, that makes war or preserves peace. The destinies of the time are enacted not in Congress or [74] Parliament, but in the Bank of England and in Wall street. It is a mighty power that sits on 'Change, and inspires the great movements of the world; sending its messengers panting through the deep and feeling around the globe with telegraphic nerves. And one may well be more ambitious to wield a portion of this power than to speak in senates, or to sit upon a throne. Here is something that will raise him above the common level; will pay him for long years of sacrifice and contumely; will hide meanness of birth, and scantiness of education, and paint over the stains of damaged character. Here is the most feasible way of distinction in a democracy. The doors of respectability and honor turn on silver hinges. Gravity relaxes, fashion gives way, beauty smiles, and talent defers, before the man of money. He may be an ignoramus, but he possesses the golden alphabet. He may be a boor, but Plutus lends a charm which eclipses the grace of Apollo. He may have accumulated his wealth in a way which would make an intelligent hyena ashamed of himself, but he *has* accumulated it, and the past is forgotten. I [75] do not mean to say that, as the general rule, wealth is thus associated, but I believe that one great motive for money-getting, is the consciousness of the power and the distinction that accompany its possession; and so, many a man in the thick dust of the mart—though it may not always be clear to himself—is really engaged in a strife for Precedence.

Again, consider the illustrations of this strife in the *Style* of *Living*. It is really a battle of chairs and mirrors, of plate and equipage, and is the spring of the monstrous extravagance that characterizes our city life. For I suppose there is no place on the earth where people have run into such gorgeous nonsense as here—turning home into a Parisian toy-shop, absorbing the price of a good farm in the ornaments of a parlor, and hanging up a judge's salary in a single chandelier. Not that I accept the standard of absolute necessity, or agree with those who cry out—"Have nothing but what is absolutely *useful!*" For, if the universe had been cast after their type, there would have been no embroidery on the wings of the butterfly, and the awful summit of Mont Blanc [76] would have yielded fire-wood. There is an instinct of beauty and grace implanted in our nature, which demands elegance and even luxury, and the bare necessaries of life do *not* answer every purpose. And, to say nothing of the employment which these accessories of refinement afford for thousands—for I have spoken of this in the previous series—the most sturdy utilitarian is not consistent with his theory. He defers to the social condition around him to such an extent that he sleeps on a bed instead of a bench, and wears broadcloth instead of untanned sheepskin. And, therefore, others might say, and say truly, that a good deal that is actually superfluous is the fruit of certain social proprieties which cannot, with any consistency, be violated. Our style of living may lawfully run from the bare necessaries of existence, through the stages of comfort and convenience, even into luxury, according to our condition and means. But in some of the style of living in this very city, there is neither good taste, social propriety, nor common sense. It is an apoplectic splendor; a melodramatic glitter; in one word, a [77] vulgar spirit of social rivalry blossoming in lace, brocade, gilding, and fresco. It is one way of getting a head taller than another upon this democratic level. It is a carpet contest for the mastery in what is called "society." And if one mourns over the exuberant selfishness that lifts its pinnacles out of this dreary sea of hunger and despair, and wonders that so many live wrapped in the idea that they were created merely to be gratified; he can hardly help being amused, on the other hand, at this fashionable strife for precedence, and the methods which it developes.

But enough has been said to illustrate the false element in the great struggle for Human Precedence. This vicious principle is most comprehensively stated in the proposition, that there is no substantial ground of supremacy in anything that is merely accidental or external to a man. These things may sometimes stand as symbols of true merit and greatness, but they are not themselves proofs of precedence. A man's wealth may be the fruit of noble energy and honest toil, and he may exert a wide influence by virtue of that [78] intrinsic ability of which his good fortune is the sign. Indeed, the more I study the world the more I acquire a respect for these kings of enterprise—these heroes of practical effort—who, feeling that they have been sent into the world to do something, do not fold their hands and shut their eyes in ideal dreams, or stumble at discrepancies, but lay hold of what lies about them—rough stone, timber, iron, brass,—and become what it is really a noble compliment to say of any man—"the architects of their own fortune." I have great respect for these men who drive the wheels, and kindle the furnaces, and launch the ships, and build the edifices, and keep this sea of every-day action perpetually agitated by the keels of their endeavor. Their claims to precedence, however, consist not in their wealth, but in that which accumulates the wealth. But the man who rests merely upon what he *has,* occupies no substantial ground of supremacy. And if this is the case with those whose claim hangs merely upon what they are worth in the world of money, it is at least equally so with those who set their title to precedence [79] upon their style of dress or living. For how uncertain are all these things! depending upon the fickle currents of fortune; throwing the honors into our hands to-day, and transferring them to our neighbor to-morrow! How tantalizing this conflict, in which victory changes with the fashion, and we feel weak or strong according to the verdict of a clique! And all these rivalries and envies and aspirations, what a confession of personal feebleness they really are! How slightly a true man feels them, who knows that he is not mere silk or furniture, and never frets about his place in the world; but just slides into it by the gravitation of his nature, and swings there as easily as a star! But the mere leader of fashion has no genuine claim to supremacy; at least, no abiding assurance of it. He has embroidered his title upon his waistcoat, and carries his worth in his watch-chain; and if he is allowed any real precedence for this it is almost a moral swindle,—a way of obtaining goods under false pretences. But without running into more minute discussion, I say again—that there is no substantial ground of [80] supremacy in aught that is merely accidental or external; and he who rests upon such claims stands upon a pedestal as uncertain as it is spurious.

"If a man strive for masteries, yet is he not crowned, except he strive lawfully." This was the old rule of the Grecian games, which would not permit the prize to be gained by any unfair or incomplete methods. It was applied by the apostle to a specific work—the great work of the Christian ministry. But it is a law which prevails in all human action. And, while it suggests that spurious precedence for which there is so much striving, it also indicates the fact that there *is* a real difference of degree among men, and that there are proper methods of obtaining supremacy.

And, as I look around in the populous city, in order to illustrate the grounds of this lawful precedence, I observe, in the first place, that there are men who occupy the higher places by ordinance of nature so to speak; or, more properly, by the purpose of God. It is a fact in nature that all men are created equal, and [81] it is also a fact in nature that all men are not equal. All men are created equal as to the essential rights and privileges of humanity. They have a claim to live; they have an impartial share in the Divine Love; they have a right to liberty, to freedom of thought and of limb, by a constitution older than any historical document, drawn up in the court of God's decrees and authenticated by His handwriting in the soul. Thus far all men are *created* equal, and, if it turns out otherwise with them, it ensues from what is *made* by man, not what is commanded by Heaven. But so far as quantity of nature is concerned—original capacity and spiritual gifts—men are not equal. And if it is asked— "Why are they not equal?" I answer, it is by appointment of the same Sovereign Mind which has ordained that "one star shall differ from another star in glory." But each form of being has its own capacities, and if these are filled the moral harmony is secured. Through all prevails the law of compensation, balancing the vicissitudes of experience. And, among these diversities of human capacity, some must [82] of necessity occupy the highest place—men whose native genius carries them up in a splendid orbit, and endows them with control. And the world at large always acknowledges the rectitude of this appointment. It cherishes no envy toward men of this kind, but renders them spontaneous homage.

But, although this genius, this original power, rises to a natural supremacy, it does not involve the most legitimate element of precedence. There is no real ground of merit in the natural talents of a man, any more than there is a ground of merit in personal beauty, or family descent. He has nothing but what has been given him— the five talents instead of his neighbor's one talent—and, so long as he does not use them to their best purpose, there is only an admirable possibility, no merit of achievement.

And all genuine merit—that which entitles one to some ground of human precedence—comes from personal achievement in life; substantially, from the stock of actual benefit which one has contributed to the world, and which has become assimilated to his own spiri

44

[83] tual nature. The ground of precedence — so far as it is lawful for man to think of anything like precedence at all — is not in outward possessions, not in gifts, but in *uses*. And here is thrown open a broad and noble field, depending not upon genius or station, but upon *will*, and therefore accessible to every man. Here is an arena where one may strive lawfully, emulous to build up his own inner nature, emulous to let such power as he possesses go out in blessings for the world. A field for all of us, my friends, right here in the dense city, amidst the hurrying feet, the clang of machinery, and the roar of wheels. And the condition of the game is, not large capacity but good purpose and loyal endeavor; not to strive greatly but to strive lawfully.

And, I observe once more, that the real claim to precedence is not eagerly snatched by us, but *comes* to us. It is not in *seeming* but in *being*, and it makes no essential difference whether the world confesses it or not, so long as we actually have it, working in our consciousness of duty and drawing our consolation from inward resources. Here, my friend, is [84] your work — here is the field of opportunity, which, however broad and rich absolutely, is for you great and pregnant with incalculable possibilities. And though men may not see its best results, they are nevertheless real, and develop in your own soul a light and power, a ground and fabric of precedence that cannot be shaken, and will never vanish away.

And yet, to a large extent, the world does confess this true supremacy. For, let me ask, who among these crowds of citizens are really honored? Not those who are so eagerly and vainly striving in their narrow, conventional circle, heedful merely of the rules of their own little game. But those who actually fill an honorable place in life. How much acknowledged dignity is there in that man who just accepts his station and makes the most of it, filling it with patience and self-sacrifice and achieving the victory of principle and affection! How much genuine nobleness in the quiet, unconscious discharge of duty! The field for precedence is it not a broad one, and close at hand? And is there no alternative between a frivolous and outside distinction, and [85] some great theatre of action large enough to fill and dazzle the world's eye? Daily, right around us, there are occasions that summon up all the energies of manhood as with a trumpet-peal. See yonder! where the conflagration, bursting through marble walls, casts a terrible splendor down the street and reddens the midnight sky. What an enemy has broken loose among us, devouring the achievements of human skill and the hopes of enterprise! What shall stay it? With a triumphant shout it snaps the fetters of stone; it roars with victory; it bends its flaming crest towards peaceful homes where men and mothers and babes lie in unconscious slumber. The bell beats; and what old bugle-strain, what pibroch, what rattling drum, ever sounded a more perilous call? And on what battle-field that you have read of was there ever displayed a loftier heroism, a more dauntless energy, than that man displays who, with the unconscious courage of duty, plunges into the furnace, mounts the quivering walls, and, making his own body a barrier between his fellow-men and the flame, stands there [86] scorched, bruised, bleeding, and beats the red terror back and beats it down, with that irresistible energy which always springs from the human will bent upon a noble purpose?

And so, in other forms, more quiet and more sacred, where the anticipation of public applause does not furnish its motive, men are exercising a heroism, and working achievements, that make dim and pale the trophies that are plucked from fields of war and in lists of glittering renown. And when these things are known the hearts of men render a spontaneous honor, and admit the genuine titles of supremacy. Yet, if this true achievement in life is not known or confessed by the world, its results really exist, and impart their inalienable strength and blessing to the soul, while as the grounds of false supremacy dissolve all gives way.

And, my friends, the tendency of things is to bring out more and more these real claims to human precedence, and to throw all spurious titles into the shade. This is the radical purport of true democracy, which I [87] take to be the social synonym of *Christianity*. I have shown what inconsistencies and false distinctions swarm here in our midst, under the profession of republican equality. This, however, is because names are *not* things. I don't call that "democracy" which is simply the domineering spirit of self-exaltation in a new shape. For there is no *essential* difference whether we call the social order a monarchy or a commonwealth; whether its leading men are Charles and Louis, or Robespierre and Cromwell. If we must have the old social fallacies, they appear more attractive with

46

the old symbols. In that case, I would rather not have them changed. For, when I look merely at the *sentimental* side of things, I feel sorry when the so-called "Royal Martyr," with a dignity which contrasts with his past conduct, stretches his head upon the block; or when the pitiless insults of a Parisian mob are hurled upon the head of the beautiful Marie Antoinette. A poetic regret and enthusiasm is awakened by the associations that cluster about the Golden Lion and the Bourbon Lilies. And, when I turn to those grim Ironsides, or those [88] frantic Jacobins, the work they are doing looks savage enough. But, with a more discriminating vision, I perceive that that rude popular storm, which desolates palaces and shatters crowns, embosoms a rectifying process which, tumbling all false distinctions from their pedestals, shall by-and-by heave up the platform of social justice, and reveal the true dignity of man. The essential work of democracy is not the destruction of forms; is not the giant arm of revolution, striking the hours of human progress by the crash of falling thrones. But its great work is *construction*—is in changing the very *spirit* of institutions—and it asserts its legitimacy and bases its claims upon the Christian doctrine of the human soul.

Therefore, I regard these spurious claims to precedence—these endeavors after social distinction by virtue of riches, and equipage, and wardrobes—as only evidences of a transition-state. Men, letting go the feudal forms, and still assuming that there is some ground of human precedence, as there really is, have adopted these false expressions of it. They [89] will in turn pass away, and give place to more genuine methods.

But let it be remembered, that these false forms of precedence are not only inconsistent with our social professions and institutions, but they are futile because they are contrary to the Divine Law. Our endeavors in life have a twofold operation, and we must count not only their effect upon others but their reaction upon the fabric of our own inner being. For, whatever honor *men* may attribute to us, we know that there is no real, substantial ground of supremacy except in the excellence and power of our own spiritual nature. And this is acquired not in ostentatious and selfish striving, but when self is least thought of; in the calm work of duty, and when all conception of human merit fades into the Glory of God. And this is the great end to be desired—this strength and exaltation of the soul.

This imparts the profoundest significance to that great life-struggle which goes on in these crowded streets. The city! what is it but a vast amphitheatre, filled with racers, with charioteers, with eager competitors; surround [90] ed by an unseen and awful array of witnesses? And here, daily, the lists are opened, and men contend for success, for station, for power. But these are meretricious and perishable awards. The real prize is a spiritual gain, a crown that "fadeth not away." And, if we comprehend the great purpose of existence at all—if we look with any eagerness to its intrinsic issues and its final result; we shall heed that decree of Divine Wisdom and Justice that comes down to us through all the vicissitude of life—through all the hurry and turmoil and contention. "If a man strive for masteries, yet is he not crowned, except he strive lawfully."

[91]

THE SYMBOLS OF THE REPUBLIC.

[92]

[93]

DISCOURSE IV.

THE SYMBOLS OF THE REPUBLIC.

Thou art a great people, and hast great power. — Joshua, xvii. 17.

These words, originally addressed by the Hebrew Leader to the children of Joseph — the tribes of Ephraim and Manasseh — have been applicable to many nations which, since that time, have risen, and flourished, and fallen. But when we consider the circumstances of its origin, its marvellous growth in all the attributes of civilization, and especially the immense *possibilities* which it involves; without even being chargeable with a natural vanity, we may say, that to no country on the face of the earth have they ever been more fitted than to this. For, my friends, we know that it *is* a dictate of our nature to magnify that which is our own. However insignificant it really is, [94] man spreads an ideal glory over the land of his birth. Perhaps its historical importance compensates for its geographical narrowness, or its material poverty is hidden by its intellectual wealth. From its stock of mighty men — its heroes, and bards, and sages — who have brightened the roll of fame; or from its memorable battle-fields, on rude heath and in mountain defile; or from its achievements which have swelled the tides of human enterprise, and made the world its debtor; he draws the inspiration, he carries away the conviction of greatness — so that wherever its emblems come before his eyes, they touch the deep springs of reverence and pride. Nor let us condemn this feeling as merely a selfish and exaggerating one. This spirit of nationality exists for wise purposes, embosoms the richest elements of loyalty and faith, and is one of those profound *sentiments* of our nature that cannot be driven out by any process of logic.

But, if a nation really inherits the description in the text, it must possess something more than an illustrious history and an ideal glory. We must determine its greatness by [95] its symbols; yet these must be not merely signs of things, but instruments of achievement; not merely the illustrations of dead works or patriotic enthusiasm, but the agents of actual power and of living performance. Now, in looking over the world at the present time, there are other nations to which the words of Joshua might be applied as well as to our own, and with as little assumption of national vanity. Other people are great and have great power, by virtue of political importance, vast possessions, and strong institutions. To say nothing of the rest, consider that huge domain which at this hour confronts the troubled principalities of Europe. It stretches itself out over three continents. The waves of three oceans chafe against its shaggy sides. The energies of innumerable tribes are throbbing in its breast. It clasps regions yet raw in history as well as those that are grey with tradition, and incloses in one empire the bones of the Siberian mammoth and the valleys of Circassian flowers. And it is great not only by geographical extent, but by political purpose — great by the idea which is involved [96] with its destiny — an idea austere as the climate, tremendous as the forces, indomitable as the will of the gigantic north. It would set the inheritance of the Byzantine Emperors in the diadem of Peter the Great. It would make the Sea of Marmara and the ridges of the Caucasus, paths to illimitable empire and uncompromising despotism. It moves down the map of the world, as a glacier moves down the Alps, patient and relentless, startling the jealous rivals that watch its course, and granting contemptuous peace to the allies that shiver in its shadow.

In considering, therefore, the symbols which prove that we also are a great people, having great power, we should select those which indicate the possession of a *peculiar* power. This peculiarity is not in our geographical extent or material greatness. But it *is*, I think, in our institutions, in the tendency of our national ideas, and in the legitimate result of these. It is in conceptions and elements the direct opposite of those that work in the destiny of the mighty empire just referred to — and for this reason I *have* referred to it.

[97]

In taking up a subject, then, which is especially connected with the conditions of humanity in the city, because in the city the conception of a people — of a public — is especially illustrated, let us inquire — What *are* the symbols of our republic; the signs and agents of our greatness as a nation? And, for the sake of avoiding too many specifications, I propose to consider these under two or three general classes.

In the first place, then, I would select as a symbol of the Republic, *Whatever represents the privilege of Free Thought.* As to whatever gives full play to the intellect, whatever diffuses the intelligence, whatever wakes up and assists the entire spiritual nature of individuals and communities, I think there is really more opportunity here than anywhere else on the face of the earth. And, as a sign and instrument of this, I would point to some *District School-house;* rough, weather-worn, standing in some bleak corner of New York or New Hampshire; through whose closed windows the passer-by catches the confused hum of recitation, or at whose door he sees [98] children of all conditions mingling in motley play. Of all conditions, so far as external peculiarities go; for the laws of nature and the ordinances of Providence cannot be dispensed with even here; but of one condition as the recognized possessors of immortal *mind.* Those who have helped mould the Republic have clearly seen that, although intelligence is not the foundation of national greatness—for there is something deeper than that—still it is the discerning and directing power upon which depends the right use even of moral elements. They have scouted the notion that there is any ultimate evil in diffused knowledge; any such thing as "a dangerous truth;" and have affirmed that the best way to winnow the false from the true, is to equip and set a-going the intellectual machine by which God has ordained that the work shall be done. It has been felt, that, if the State can properly extend its influence anywhere beyond the restrictive limits of evil, or the punishment of overt wrong; if anywhere it may exercise a positive ministration for good; it is here, where it does not interfere on the one hand [99] with those outward pursuits which should be left to individual choice and aptitude, nor on the other, with those inward sanctities which pertain to conscience and to God; it is here, in that region of our personality from which we can best discern our duty and fill our place. For the intellect is the most neutral of all our qualities. Man is swayed by the animal propensities of his nature; he is swayed by the moral and religious elements of his nature; but the intellect, by itself, is not a motive power. It is a *light;* and no one will object to its being kindled except those who, by that objection, virtually confess that they fear the light. And this work of kindling is just what the state purposes to do for a child; leaving his religious convictions to such helps as conscience has chosen, and his position in life to the decision of circumstances. And there is no way in which it can show so much impartiality, and exercise practically the most essential conception of freedom. For thus, as I have already said, it recognizes a common inheritance—something which all have—the possession of *mind*—something which is of [100] more importance than any external condition, for it influences external condition; (whoever saw an educated community of which anything like a large fraction were paupers and criminals?) something on which rests the claim of human freedom; for the charter of man's liberty is in his soul, not his estate. It says to the poorest child—"You are rich in this one endowment, before which all external possessions grow dim. No piled-up wealth, no social station, no throne, reaches as high as that spiritual plane upon which every human being stands by virtue of his humanity; and from that plane, mingling now in the Common School with the lowliest and the lordliest, we give you the opportunity to ascend as high as you may. We put into your hands the key of knowledge; leaving your religious convictions, with which we dare not interfere, to your chosen guides. So far as the intellectual path may lead, it is open to you.—Go free!" And when we consider the great principles which are thus practically confessed; when we consider the vast consequences which grow out of this; I think that little District School-house [101] dilates, grows splendid, makes our hearts beat with admiration and gratitude, makes us resolve that at all events, *that* must stand; for, indeed, it is one of the noblest symbols of the Republic—a sign and an instrument of a great people, having great power.

Or, if you would behold another of these symbols, go through this city, and pause wherever you hear the rumbling of the *Printing-Press*. As I have dwelt upon the characteristics of this great power in another place, I only allude to it here as a vehicle of that *expression* which is so essential to all genuine freedom of thought. Mere education is no evidence of this freedom. It may be made, it has been made in one of the most intelligent but despotic countries in Europe, an instrument for drilling the human mind into an absolute routine of state policy. Mere liberty of speculation is nothing, though it has the boundless firmament of abstraction for its own, so long as it is not allowed to strike the solid ground of fact or touch one organized abuse. Let us be thankful for a free-press—the electric tongue of thought, which at every stroke is felt [102] throughout a continent, which no dictator dares to chain, and over whose issues no censor sits in judgment—or only that great censor, public opinion. Everybody is aware of its evil as well as its good—the errors, the crudities, the abominations it sends out. But we must remember that it is only the representative, the voice, of elements that actually exist in human minds and bosoms; and, surely, it is better that they should come out into the free air, and be sprinkled by the chloride of truth, than to work darkly and infectiously out of sight. It is the hidden, not the open evil that is dangerous.

Or, still again, you might have seen a true symbol of the Republic in the spectacle which has been presented this very day—the spectacle of a *Free Worship*. The great stream of religious impulse has poured through these streets, and separated into its rills of distinctive opinion, without trepidation and without challenge. Every man has had the opportunity to commune with his God, and approach the Cross of his Redeemer, with no established barriers between. Neither the cathedral nor [103] the chapel rest upon the patronage of the state, but in the deep foundations of individual conviction. To be sure, here and there, there is a little assumption; but it is dramatic rather than substantial, and does not amount to much. Here and there breaks out an unjust prejudice or a spiteful calumny, but it shames the source more than the object, and soon dies away in the atmosphere of tolerance and investigation. It looks doubtful sometimes, but I verily believe that the real spirit, as well as the mere form of Religious equality, is beginning to prevail. Every day, it is more and more practically acknowledged that Christianity is profounder than any name, and exists under strange and despised names; that there really is decent observance in every church, and holy living in every communion; and a man finds that his neighbor has the same essence of righteousness as himself, though he has not half so many links in his creed. And something more than tolerance grows out of this practical liberty. It is not easy to measure the moral sincerity, the moral principle, which results from it; which is far more precious than mere [104] intelligence; which is the perennial spring and assurance of national welfare.

But I proceed to observe, in the second place, that we may select as a symbol of the Republic—a sign and an instrument of a great people, having great power—whatever illustrates the principle of *Political Equality*. I am speaking, at present, not of our deficiencies, but of our possessions; not of the instances in which this doctrine of equality is practically contradicted, but of those in which it is practically acknowledged. The sovereignty of every man is a fundamental principle in our institutions; it is essential to the conception of a Republic; and so far as it *is* legitimately a Republic, we shall find this principle in operation. And, looking around for some extant symbol of this, let me select that which is the object of so much strife and agitation—the *Presidential Chair*. I do not, by any means, consider this the most comfortable seat in the nation, or that the most deserving man is sure to get there; but, as an emblem, I believe it illustrates the noblest privileges, and the proudest supremacy, on the face of the globe. [105] And I refer to it as a *possibility* for the poorest and humblest child in the land. No hereditary gallery leads to it—only the broad road of the people. And, as the highest seat in the nation, it illustrates all the honors of the nation. They are possible to anybody. And I trust the time has not yet arrived when this can be said only by way of satire; can be true only because the waves of political corruption carry the meanest and unworthiest into office; but as a grand fact, a fact with which are involved the springs of our national greatness and power, it may be said that here there are no barriers of caste, no terms of descent, no depths so low that enterprise cannot rise out of them, no heights so exalted that genius cannot attain them; for, on a platform as level to the peasant's threshold as to the nabob's door, stand the judge's bench, the senator's seat, and the President's chair.

As another symbol of this political equality, I would name the *Ballot-Box*. I am aware that this is not everywhere a consistent symbol; but to a large degree it is so. I know what miserable associations cluster [106] around this instrument of popular power. I know that the arena in which it stands is trodden into mire by the feet of reckless ambition and selfish greed. The wire-pulling and the bribing, the pitiful truckling and the grotesque compromises, the exaggeration and the detraction, the melo-dramatic issues and the sham patriotism, the party watch-words and the party nick-names, the schemes of the few paraded as the will of the many, the elevation of men whose only worth is in the votes they command—vile men, whose hands you would not grasp in friendship, whose presence you would not tolerate by your fireside—incompetent men, whose fitness is not in their capacity as functionaries, or legislators, but as organ pipes; the snatching at the slices and offal of office, the intemperance and the violence, the finesse and the falsehood, the gin and the glory; these are indeed but too closely identified with that political agitation which circles around the Ballot-Box. But, after all, they are not essential to it. They are only the masks of a genuine grandeur and importance. For it *is* a grand thing— [107] something which involves profound doctrines of Right—something which has cost ages of effort and sacrifice—it *is* a grand thing that here, at last, each voter has just the weight of one man; no more, no less; and the weakest, by virtue of his recognized manhood, is as strong as the mightiest. And consider, for a moment, what it is to cast a vote. It is the token of inestimable privileges, and involves the responsibilities of an hereditary trust. It has passed into your hands as a right, reaped from fields of suffering and blood. The grandeur of History is represented in your act. Men have wrought with pen and tongue, and pined in dungeons, and died on scaffolds, that you might obtain this symbol of freedom, and enjoy this consciousness of a sacred individuality. To the ballot have been transmitted, as it were, the dignity of the sceptre and the potency of the sword. And that which is so potent as a right, is also pregnant as a duty; a duty for the present and for the future. If you will, that folded leaf becomes a tongue of justice, a voice of order, a force of imperial law; securing rights, [108] abolishing abuses, erecting new institutions of truth and love. And, *however* you will, it is the expression of a solemn responsibility, the exercise of an immeasurable power for good or for evil, now and hereafter. It is the medium through which you act upon your country—the organic nerve which incorporates you with its life and welfare. There is no agent with which the possibilities of the Republic are more intimately involved, none upon which we can fall back with more confidence, than the Ballot-Box.

But there is a symbol which represents the power and greatness of a Republic more significantly than all the rest, and is comprehensive of all the rest. It is the fruit of unfettered thought and political equality, of intelligence and virtue, of private sovereignty and public duty—it is a free, true, harmonious *Man*. As the crown or the sceptre is the symbol of a Monarchy; as heraldic honors are the symbols of an Oligarchy; so, I repeat, the most expressive symbol of a Republic is a man—a man free in limb and soul, a man intelligent and self-governed, a [109] man whose spiritual vision is clear, and in whose breast the voice of conscience is peremptory, with whom the conception of duties is deeper even than the conception of rights; in short, a man who embodies all the elements, and represents to the world the best results of Liberty. Laws are nothing, institutions are nothing, national power and greatness are nothing, save as they assist the Moral purpose of God in the development of humanity. To this test we must bring the symbols of the Republic, and judge whether they are fitting and consistent. No matter what else they accomplish, no matter what else they signify, if they do not serve this end they are either incomplete instruments, or vain forms. For, Man is of more worth than Institutions; Religion is greater than politics; and the designs of Providence are wider than the cycles of National destiny.

I turn, then, to the signs of our own national greatness; I turn to these symbols of spiritual freedom and political equality; and I ask—how completely do they develop this most significant symbol of all—how completely do [110] they serve the purposes of God in History—by securing the welfare, the culture, the moral elevation of humanity? And the reply is—that, by our institutions and our endeavors, these ends have been served in various ways. There is here, to-day, a more enlightened, free, self-governed humanity—and we say it without arrogance—than anywhere else on the globe. Our benefits are of the kind that are not realized, because they are so great and familiar—like the light and the air; but take them away, or transfer us to some other atmosphere, and how we should miss them, and pine and dwindle! Let no man, in his zeal for bold rebuke or needed reform, overlook what has been done, and what is enjoyed here, as to the noblest results of national greatness and power.

But every sincere man must say likewise that, with us, the *possibilities* are far greater than the *performance*; that these symbols are the splendid tokens of what *may be*, rather than what *is*. And, that I may bring this discourse to a practical conclusion, let me say that two things, at least, are necessary to con [111] vert these possibilities into the noblest achievement.

In the first place, it is essential that every citizen of the republic should recognize his own manhood; the sacredness of his own personality; and should recognize this especially in relation to his duties, which are inextricably involved with his rights. For here it is true in a special sense, that the mass is but an aggregate of personalities—that public sin is but the projection of your sin and mine. A man will often say that he is responsible to his country, and responsible to his constituents; but upon no claim, by no sophistry, should he suffer himself to forget that he is also responsible to his God. He does forget this, when he acts for political interests, and as one of a party, as he never would act in his private affairs. And does he suppose that there is a corporate vice, or virtue, differing from his private vice or virtue, as a gentleman's purse differs from the public fund? There is no such distinction in moral qualities. It is your own coin that helps swell the amount; it bears your stamp, and you are responsible for the [112] product. If the party lies, then *you* are guilty of falsehood. If the party—as is very likely—does a mean thing, then *you* do it. It is surely so, so far as you are one of the party, and go with it in its action. God does not take account of parties; party names are not known in that court of Divine Judgment; but your name and mine are on the books there. There is no such thing—and this is true, perhaps, in more senses than one—there is no such thing as a party conscience. It is individual conscience that is implicated. Party! Party! Ah! my friends, here is the influence which, it is to be feared, balks and falsifies many of these glorious symbols. Men rally round musty epithets. They take up issues which have no more relation to the deep, vital, throbbing interest of the time, than they have to the fashions of our grandfathers. They parade high-sounding principles to cover selfish ends; interpret the Constitution by a doctrine of loaves and fishes; while individual independence and private conviction are whirled away in the political maelstrom, and the party-badge is reverenced and hugged as the [113] African reverences and hugs his fetish. And surely it is a case for congratulation, when some great, exciting question breaks out and jars these conventional idols, and so sweeps and shatters these party organizations and turns them topsy-turvy, that a man is shaken out of his harness, does not know exactly what party he *does* belong to, and begins to feel that he has a soul of his own. I am not denying the use and the necessity of parties as instruments, but

protest against them as ends, especially when principle is smoth-
ered under their platforms, and they absorb the moral personality of
a man.

It may not seem so strange that the political field should so often
be the field of a lax and depressed morality, when we consider that
here is the great theatre where human ambition struggles for its
aims; here are enlisted the strongest passions of the soul; here
throng some of its fiercest temptations; here the stakes played for
are the kingdoms of this world, and the glory of them. And this, I
suppose, is the reason why the most authentic type of human depravity is a thoroughly [114] unprincipled politician. Such an instance, at least, may strike us more forcibly, because we see the
perversion of great faculties, and capabilities are contrasted with
performance; while, on the other hand he may be confirmed in his
moral bankruptcy by the fact that, in playing upon the passions of
men he sees the worst side of humanity. But, surely, there have
been those who passed this ordeal, and came out with brighter lus-
tre; who have kept the eye of conscience elevated above the ecliptic
of political routine; who have made politics identical with lofty
duties and great principles; whose patriotism was not a clamorous
catch-word, but a breathing inspiration, a silent heart-fire. In private
life they have felt the great privilege of their citizenship; the magnitude of the obligation which bound them to virtue and to consistency; while, in public life, they have kept their trust firm as steel,
bright as gold; have felt, with due balance on either side, the beat-
ings of the popular heart and the dictates of the everlasting Right;
and in themselves have represented the union of liberty and law,
the real greatness of a [115] nation. Without such men, the nation
has no greatness; for its significance and its power are in the moral
worth of its citizens.

The second condition necessary to the fulfilment of the great results indicated by these symbols, is consistent action upon the ideas
that constitute the basis of our own institutions. If many of the privileges and peculiarities which I have specified in this discourse are
possessed by other nations, in one respect we differ from them all.
These privileges and peculiarities are *legitimately* ours. They have
not been grafted on hereditary antagonisms. They have not grown
up in *spite* of our institutions, but as the *fruit* of our institutions.

These ideas, entwined with the very roots of our Republic, shooting through every fibre, running into every limb, bind us to a recognition of human brotherhood; to sympathy with Liberty wherever it struggles; and to stedfast opposition to whatever crushes the rights, hinders the development, or denies the humanity of man. If these symbols of the Republic mean anything, they mean just this; and whatever is inconsistent with this, is [116] inconsistent with the terms of our national birthright. Depend upon it, not the assertion of Liberty, but whatever is opposed to Liberty, is the innovating and agitating element in this country. It interrupts the legitimate current of our destiny. It shocks the popular heart with inconsistency. It becomes mixed with the ashes of the old heroes, and the land keeps heaving with the fermentation. One assumption is too impudent, too nakedly in contradiction with the fundamental ideas of our Republic ever to be admitted—the assumption that the man who speaks for freedom, who sympathizes with the broadest doctrine of human rights, and sets around these the eternal barriers of justice, is an innovator and an agitator. I ask—what made our Revolution legitimate? What were the central ideas that throbbed in the breasts of its heroes and martyrs? Take down the old muskets bent in the hot encounter, and printed with many a death-gripe; take down the old uniforms, clipped by Hessian sabres and torn by British bullets; take down the dusty muster-rolls, scrawled with those venerable names—names [117] that now "are graven on the stone," names that are buried in the sod, names that have gone up to immortality—and ask, for what was this great struggle? Was it not for freedom, based upon the conception of the right and supremacy of freedom? And is *this* the legitimate conclusion of that sublime postulate—this other Fact which, never retreating, always advancing, follows the steps of Freedom over the continent like a shadow, looms up like a phantom against the Rocky Mountains, and darkens the fairest waters? On the contrary, is not Freedom that old truth, that conceded premise that does *not* agitate? Liberty, Human Rights, Universal Brotherhood, was it not for these ideas ye fought—was it not these ye planted in the soil, and laid with the corner-stone of our institutions? My friends, I know, and you know, could those men give palpable sign and representation, the answer that would come, as in one quick flash from bayonet to bayonet, in one long roll of drums, from Lexington to Yorktown.

These peculiar privileges, then, to which I have referred, differ from those of other [118] nations inasmuch as they are not grafted expedients, but legitimate fruits. Unless we change the premises of our Republic, and shift the foils in our historical argument, these are necessary conclusions. They are necessary conclusions, if our symbols represent realities. Russia is consistent with its national idea. It pours forth its legions and moves to its work with a terrible consistency. And if we—also a great people, having great power—are equally consistent, we shall fall back upon no selfish conservatism, but aid whatever tends to fulfil the Providential purpose of our existence, and whatever helps and advances man.

One thing is certain. So long as any nation truly lives, it unfolds its specific idea and lives according to its original type. When it fails to do this, the sentence of decay is already written upon it. If it fails to illustrate God's purpose in its obedience, it illustrates His control in retribution. For there is nothing supreme, nothing finally triumphant, nothing of the last importance, but His Law. It penetrates, and oversweeps, and survives all charters and institutions and nationalities, [119] like the infinite space that encompasses Alps and Andes, and planets and systems. It is this that successive generations illustrate. It is this that all history vindicates. If a nation runs parallel to this Divine Law, it is well; if false to its purpose and its control, down it goes. The prophet Isaiah, in one of the most terrific and sublime passages of the Bible, represents the king of Babylon, while passing into the under-world, saluted by departed rulers, by dead kings, rising from their shadowy thrones, and exclaiming, "Art thou become weak as we? Art thou become like unto us?" Thus has many a nation gone down to its doom. Shall it be so with this Republic, because false to its ideal? Shall it descend to the shades of perished pomp and greatness, and see Nineveh with dusty, hieroglyphic robes rising up to meet it; and Persia, with the empty winecup of its luxury; and Rome, with the shadow of universal empire on its discrowned head; and hear them say—"Art thou become weak as we? Art thou become like unto us?"

My friends, I look at the eager enterprise, [120] the young, hopeful vigor, the tides of possibility that flow through this great city; I look at the symbols of this Republic; and I cannot believe that such is to be the result. I look back upon our history, and cannot argue such a future from such a past. A great light lay upon the wake of those frail ships that bore our fathers hither; the wake of past ages, the following of good men's prayers and brave men's deeds, the mingling currents of martyr-blood and prophet-fire. And methinks, as they struck the shore, and met the savage wilderness, a Voice saluted them; a voice not of profane ambition and of selfish hope, but of Divine promise, intending Divine results—proclaiming, "Thou art a great people, and hast great power." And He will fulfil this prophecy, Who leads the course of history over the broad deep and through mysterious ways, and Who unfolds His own glory in the destinies of men.

[121]

THE SPRINGS OF SOCIAL LIFE.

[122]

[123]

DISCOURSE V.

THE SPRINGS OF SOCIAL LIFE.

Let them learn first to show piety at home. — I. Timothy, v. 4.

The text — which I purpose to employ not as a specific precept, but as the illustration of a general principle — indicates those Springs of Social Life which constitute the subject of the present discourse.

The crowd in a city affords comparatively little interest, when we contemplate it merely as a crowd. But, when we resolve it into its individual particles, and consider each of these as endued with the attributes and involved with the conditions of humanity, our deepest sympathies are touched. Every drop of that great stream is a conscious personality. In some shape, the universe is reflected in it. In some way, it takes hold of the reality of life: [124] and the living organism of which it is composed both acts and suffers, receives from the world around it and contributes to it. That entire mass of people involves nothing more than the interest of humanity, and the same interest pertains to the least unit of that mass.

And, doubtless, you have sometimes busied yourself with the speculation — "Where do all these people come from? And whither do they retire at night?" Now, this is really a very suggestive question, and to follow it out to a practical answer would yield results of the profoundest importance. For out of hidden channels, here and there, *do* spring all these struggling activities, these human diversities, these various influences good and evil, that make up the crowd and spectacle of city life. And night after night, with the rarest exceptions, into some retreat they all disappear. Some spot — whether it seem the veriest mockery to style it so, or whether it be a synonym for the sweetest sanctities — some spot each of this living multitude calls by the name of "Home."

For some that name is associated with a [125] more than oriental magnificence. Man and nature wait upon them there in every conceivable form of service. There is no method of convenience or luxury which ingenuity can devise; no bounty that earth can yield from her many-zoned bosom; no shape which art can summon from the regions of the beautiful, that is not possible there. Lifting its palatial walls, and kindling with brilliant lights, it stands there as the completest symbol of material refinement and civilization. It is arctic winter without. The snow chokes up the dreary street, and the whistling wind cuts the beggar's rags. But it is Italy, it is Ceylon, it is tropic gorgeousness within. And these are the abodes of the children of fortune, whose wishes require no talisman but expression, who, all their lives long, have been used to such indulgence, or who accept it now as the fruit of their own effort. This is the hospitality which some men find in life, and out of which they constitute a home.

But none the less enviable, and perhaps much more so, are those retreats where comfort waits on moderate means, while contentment [126] imparts to these an unpurchasable efficacy; where, blended with those infirmities and liabilities which are common to palace and cottage, the domestic affections flourish, and the dearest treasures of life are kept. Thousands of homes like this there are, all around us. It describes the largest class of homes, we may believe. And who can estimate their influence over these busy tides of action, all day long? That world of traffic, that world of toil, that looks so hard and gross and sordid, — is it not transformed somewhat, does it not grow beautiful even, when you think how many of its energies have their spring by the infant's cradle and the mother's chair? And what lights, what shadows, unseen by you, fall upon the speculative eyes, fall upon the hearts, of thousands in that homeward-streaming crowd! Light of welcoming hearth-fires, shadows of children's play upon the walls; light of affections in which there are no decay and no deceit; shadows of sacred retirement where God alone is; light of joys which this world's storms cannot utterly quench; shadows of sorrow around sick-beds, and in vacant [127] places, that still make home the dearer as the arena of earth's purest discipline and of its most triumphant faith!

And why delineate the features of that other class of homes, whose most significant word is *"Privation?"* Where cheerlessness, and hunger, and desponding toil, or hopeless apathy, brood continually. Let your own sympathies, let your own imaginations that cannot exaggerate the reality, call up the vision of such. Think how many such abodes there are this very night, which winter besieges with all his terrors, and into which he sends his invading frost!

Think what Home is to hundreds, and, therefore, how life looks to them, seen through this atmosphere of disease and want, with starvation by the hearth, and death at the door, and misery everywhere! Think, when the cold pierces even through all your wrappages of comfort, and scarcity almost pinches, what forms of humanity, with lungs, and nerves, and hearts, and every capacity for suffering, are scraping the moss of subsistence from the barest rocks of life, and struggling every day through an [128] avalanche! Think what this Sabbath has been in the dwellings of the poor, you who have had time to listen to the Gospel, and have heard it comfortably — so comfortably, perhaps, that you have fallen asleep under it — think what this Sabbath has been in the dwellings of the poor! And yet, when I consider what, doubtless, the Sabbath has been in some of those places, I am thankful that the highest ideal, the richest sanctities of Home, are not dependent upon outward conditions; for even there, unfaltering duty and true love have made the bare walls beautiful, and prayer has set the desolate chamber on the steps of the Divine throne; and before the eye of faith the cold arch of the winter night, that looks in through hole and cranny, has burst into a revelation of heaven, and a path for those ministering angels that come to help the sufferer and to comfort God's poor.

With more unqualified sadness, therefore, our thoughts must rest upon still another group of dwellings, where deprivation and ignorance are mingled with vice and crime — where want and guilt strip away the masks of [129] civilization, and bring out the essential savage in man's nature. These also we must call "*homes*!" These breathing-holes of abomination, these moral tombs, where huddle the demons of violence, and cunning, and debauchery, and from which they issue. That vast Hades of social evil opening downward from our streets, where the best ideals have no type, and the purest sentiments scarce a name; where God is but a dark cloud of muttering thunder in the soul; where all that is fair in womanhood is dishevelled and transformed; and where childhood is baptized in infamy, trained to sin, canopied with curses, and rocked to sleep by the convulsive hell of passions all around it.

The Homes of the Metropolis! Thus diversified are they in their general types, and more numerous in their individual conditions than can be specified. And, surely, it is no vain speculation that inquires—"What are they? Into what retreats do the elements of this busy crowd dissolve, night after night?" Whatever they may be, a common interest envelopes them and links them all together— [130] the interest of humanity. They have vanished from the streets. One great shadow covers them, and hides their distinctions. For a time they are all equal. They have fallen asleep—poor, tired humanity at the best!—they have fallen asleep on the bosom of a common Providence, that bears them all up, as it bears the planet on which they now repose, through the orbit of its great purpose and the immensities of its love. But in the morning all these diversities will break forth again, each pouring its influence into the general stream. And who does not perceive how much the character of that influence must depend upon the condition of those homes? Who does not see that not only the interest of the common humanity in its most intimate experiences attaches to them, but the interest of community? Not only are they the reservoirs of individual power and peculiarity, but they are the Springs of Social Life. And this the apostle indicated, when he directed that certain, who bore intimate relations to the early church, should "first learn to show piety at home."

Keeping this conclusion in mind, let me ask [131] you to consider, for a little while, what Home *must* be.

In the first place—it is the *earliest and the most influential school.* Nowhere else is the character so moulded; nowhere else is so much infused into our entire being. For, whatever it may be, it is the nursery of childhood; and "the child is father to the man." Here dawns upon the human mind the conception of life. Here, when the nature is uninscribed and plastic, it takes its first impressions. I suppose it to be true, that more is learnt, more that is elementary and a key to all the rest, in the first few years of childhood than in all after time. I do not deny, of course, that much is corrected and overcome under another class of influences. But the deepest impressions, the seeds of the most stubborn habits, are planted at home. Hence the peculiar anxiety of good men to rescue *children* from the influences of a bad home. And, even then, with what obstacles do they have to contend! How radical are the prejudices already formed in that young mind! How obstinate the customs, how opaque the [132] ignorance, how rank the growth of error! Nay, into what complete fruition have all these grown, simply in the neglect of home-culture, to say nothing of influences positively evil! Really, the color and current of a man's destiny are indicated here, unless a shock of wonderful transformation comes over him. I do not mean to say that anybody is wholly the creature of circumstances; but he is the *subject* of circumstances. If they do not entirely make *him*, they furnish the occasion out of which he makes something; and, viewed either from the platform of the inward or the outward, they furnish an important key to his life. And, although the path of reformation is more difficult than the descent into evil, and demands an effort which too few are inclined to put forth; though by the conditions of our nature the good is more easily swept away than the bad; still, it is encouraging to estimate the permanence and the power of those *good* influences which are received at home. Everybody knows, when he is pitched into this whirlpool of evil that rolls around him in the world, how those old [133] home-restraints lie upon him like a magic chain, hard to be forced away—perhaps never utterly forced away. And, seeking for those who should stand up in this boisterous sweep of sin, you would look and I would look to those who had received the best impressions under the domestic roof. If I were alone, poor, compelled to ask charity somewhere in this selfish world, I would go, not to the man who has learnt most of what he calls his "wisdom" from the experience of mature life, but to him in whose heart there evidently remains something of childhood's tenderness, kept warm by the remembered pressures of his mother's breast. If I were seeking to restore some wild prodigal, brazen-fronted by his own wicked will and by the scorn with which men have battered him—if I were looking for some gleam of promise in his turbulent nature, and sounding its depths to find some spring of repentance—I should never despair if I could discover one gentle pulse that beat with the memories of a good and happy home. Why, who needs to be told of the potency of this our earliest school, to say [134] nothing of other influences, if only a faithful *mother* presides there? O! mother, mother, name for the earliest relationship, symbol of the divine tenderness; kindling a love that we never blush to confess, and a veneration that we cannot help rendering; how does your mystic influence, imparted from the soft pressure and the undying smile, weave itself through all the brightness through all the darkness of our after life. The mould of character set on the front of the world's great men, and gladly confessed by them, bears your stamp. Your inspiration burns along the poet's line. It is your true courage, more than man's rude daring, that makes the force of heroes. The statesman, when treason to humanity wears the garb of power, and duty calls him like a trumpet, hears your voice. The philanthropist, when he feels that the most efficient service is to be patient and to wait, imbibes the strength of your fortitude. The sailor, "on the high and giddy mast," mingles your name close to God's. And thousands in life's great claims, in life's great perils, trace back the influences of the hour to [135] some early time, some calm moment, when, — little, timid children, — they knelt by your side, and from tones of reverence and looks of love and simple words of prayer, they first learnt piety at home.

But I observe again, that Home is the sphere where are most clearly displayed *the real elements of character*. The world furnishes occasions of trial, but it also furnishes prudential considerations. Without any absolute hypocrisy, one measures his speech and restrains his action in the street and the market. And it is easy to conceive how small men may perform great deeds, and mean men seem philanthropic, and cowards flourish as heroes, with the tremendous motive of publicity to urge them. But at home all masks are thrown aside, and the true proportions of the man appear. Here he can find his actual moral standard, and measure himself accordingly. If he is irritable, here breaks forth his repressed fretfulness. If he is selfish, here are the sordid tokens. If he passes in any way for more than he is worth, here you may detect the counterfeit in the ring of his natural voice and the superscription [136] of his undisguised life. No, the world is not the place to prove the moral stature and quality of a man. There are too many props and stimulants. Nor, on the other hand, can he himself determine his actual character merely by looking into his own solitary heart. Therein he may discover *possibilities*, but it needs actuality to make up the estimate of a complete life. He must *do* something as well as be something; he must do something in order that he may be something. For, what he thinks is in his heart may be exaggerated by self-flattery, or darkened by morbid self-distrust. It needs some occasion to prove what is really there. And Home is precisely that sphere which is sufficiently removed from the factitious motives of publicity on the one extreme, and the unexercised possibilities of the human heart on the other, to afford a genuine test. What a man really is, therefore, will appear in the truest light under his own roof and by his own fireside. I can believe that he is a Christian, when I know that he faithfully takes up the daily duties, and bears the crosses, that cluster within his own doors. [137] I shall think that the world rightly calls him a philanthropist, when, notwithstanding common faults and infirmities, he receives the spontaneous award of the good husband and father, and the kindness of his nature is reflected in the very air and light of his dwelling. And,—talk of noble deeds!—where will you find occasions for, where will you behold manifestations of, a more beautiful self-sacrifice, a more generous heroism, than in the labors and in the endurance of thousands of men and women, shut out from the world's observation in silent nooks and corners of this very city, amidst the relationships and cares and struggles of home? But whether it be in forms of good or evil, we know that the real elements of character, the genuine moral qualities of people, must be expressed there.

And, I remark once more, that at Home we must find *the most essential happiness or misery of life.* The same conditions apply here as those which relate to character. The world is a theatre of *seeming,* and we can hardly tell by what we notice there who is, or who is not, happy. We know that gaiety is [138] often the reckless ripple over depths of despair; and that men will bear up with a smile while untold agony is gnawing at their heart-strings, and will die laughing, in an agony of defiance, under the sword-strokes of fortune. On the other hand we may count some as unfortunate, in whose bosoms, all the while, there are flowing inexhaustible springs of peace, and who derive real joy from what we suppose to be a hard and pitiable lot. But amidst the undisguised realities of home we can form the most correct estimate of a man's condition. In the first place because, as has been remarked, he is there most truly himself. He gains opportunity for reflection, and gives vent to the secret burden of his heart. There he empties the load of his envies, his rivalries, his disappointments; which he has carried before the world muffled in courtesy or pride. These, it may be, meet and are re-acted upon by kindred elements; engendered, perhaps, by the very atmosphere which he himself, in the first place, created. Oh! how many rich dwellings there are, crowded with every appointment of luxury, that are only glittering [139] ice-caverns of selfishness and discontent; pavilions of misery, where jangling discord mars the show, and a chill of mutual distrust breathes through the sumptuous apartments, and heartless ostentation presides like a robed skeleton at the feast. You feel that nothing is genial or spontaneous there. The courtesy is dreary etiquette, and the laughter forced music. You would dine as happily with the forms on the canvas, with the cold marbles in the hall. For all this magnificence is nothing more than a gorgeous pall over dead affections—nothing more than the coronation of a living woe.

"Better is a dinner of herbs," says the wise man, "where love is, than a stalled ox and hatred therewith." And many a home exists where there *is* but little more than a dinner of herbs, which affection and mutual loyalty, and sweet dispositions, convert into a palace. And there are fixed boundaries of peace, that society cannot encroach upon, while the processions of ambition and pleasure and ceaseless pursuit, pass by its windows and disturb it not. Here the good man and [140] the brave man—the man who has nobly discharged his duty at whatever cost—is respected and understood. Hither he can retreat beyond the shots of calumny which have torn the ensign of his good name; beyond the deceit of men, which halts at the threshold. Here he can look calmly out upon the changes of fortune and the frowns of the world. Here his perplexed spirit finds inspirations of strength, and space for rest. There is no happiness in life, there is no misery, like that growing out of the dispositions which consecrate or desecrate a Home.

Moreover, the elements of profoundest joy or suffering are there, because there are unfolded the deepest experiences of our mortal lot. There transpire those events which constitute the *eras* of our existence. There, day by day, grows the sentiment of filial veneration and love. There is the joy of wedded felicity. There wells up in the heart the first strange gush of parental affection. There comes the intimation of awful change staring upon us with the face of [141] death. There falls the shadow of the funeral train, passing across the threshold. There breaks in upon us the sense of bereavement, in the vacant chambers; where the familiar foot-step patters, where the familiar voice is heard no more. From the very nature of things, the profoundest happiness and misery of human life must be experienced among the conditions of Home.

Having thus in some respects considered what Home *must* be, I have virtually anticipated whatever may be said in the second division of this discourse respecting what Home *ought* to be.

Thus, as it is the earliest and most influential school, it behoves every one who is bound by its responsibilities to make it an agent of the *best culture.* The great subject of Home Education, is of itself enough for a series of discourses; and I have not room to lay down even the general propositions which belong to it, much less for specifications. But I would remind you—and I think the suggestion is especially needed amidst the whirl of city life—that there *is* such a thing as Home [142] Education, and it presses its claims upon everybody who inhabits a Home. There is such a thing as Home Education, differing from school education, whether of the week day or the Sabbath, and therefore it is a matter we ought to attend to, and not suppose we have done enough when we patronize an academy, or help fill a class on Sunday. To every parent—to every influential member of a household—there is committed a charge which can be shifted to no one else; there is an opportunity which no outside teacher possesses. There are some duties in life that we have to look for and to go after; there are others which are passed right into our hands, whether we will or not. And this duty of Home Education is of the latter kind. Now, I have just said that I cannot specify here, and even if there were room I am not sure that it would be advisable. For I doubt whether we can give any manual of methods and instruments in this respect, any more than there can be a manual of religious exercises suited to every spiritual peculiarity. Dispositions, capacities, circumstances, must [143] create their own methods. And perhaps the poorest method of all would be some system of domestic education, which the experimenter thinks will do the work exactly. I am somewhat suspicious of systems. I am more than suspicious of any constrained formal method, bringing up children in a mere manual drill, crimping them into a mould of mincing proprieties, and making them speak with an automaton click. Perhaps the most headlong young men that can be found, are those who spent their early days in a sort of strait jacket with a clock-work movement. They were wound up so tight when they were boys, that now they take great pleasure in going fast, and running down. In other words, having felt their early training to be mere *training*, the moment they strip off the constraint, they plunge into the opposite extreme of *no* constraint. Nay, I believe that even children who are left to their own instincts, and shoved out into the world to take care of themselves, are generally better balanced, and go with steadier motion than these. Of course, however, neither extreme is right. [144] There is such a thing, I say once more, as Home Education, involving all necessary training and true constraint; and yet not oppressively felt as such, because it is free, informal, and respects the spontaneity of the childish nature. But, whether our Home Education be formal or informal, direct or indirect, there is one kind of education which we are sure to impart. It is the education of example, silent, effective, stronger and more easily apprehended than any set of maxims. I would we were all duly impressed with the responsibilities of Home as they appear in this light; might feel, however we may be absorbed in business or in pleasure, that the young mind and heart are receiving influences, and growing into expressions that in some way will surprise us.

In the next place I observe, that if we display our real dispositions and characters at home, we should recognize it practically as *a sphere of moral discipline*. The family is a divine ordinance—the Home is an institution of God, forecast in the peculiarities of our very nature. History shows no period [145] when it did not exist, and we discover no tribe so barbarous as to be without it. It is the foundation of all society. It embosoms the germ and ideal of the State. According to the purity of its relations, the intensity of its sympathies, the inviolability of its rights, a nation's life is high or low, feeble or strong, fickle or enduring. And if it is thus rooted in the nature and the history of man, we may well believe that it affords some of the profoundest occasions for that moral discipline which is the great purpose of our existence upon the earth.

It is certainly the great sphere in which our affections are to be cultivated. Of course I do not mean that this is the limit of their cultivation. But here they are nurtured, and out of this they grow. As love is the Infinite Nature itself, so is it the prevalent sentiment of all life. It has been ordained that this great element should flow through every form of being, linking them together by a common feeling, and lending some interest to the most insignificant. And man has been set in the family relation that this [146] sentiment might be developed. There is no one in whose heart it does not exist. You cannot find me a being so defaced, so alienated from the common stock of humanity, as to cherish in his bosom no secret fount of love, no fibril of affection linking him to something else. But of this love there are numerous degrees; and the highest forms of it, that go forth in expressions of self-sacrifice and worldwide sympathy, are only developed by culture. And for this culture there are rich opportunities amidst the relations and sanctities of Home.

And there is opportunity among these relations also, for active duty, and in its daily tasks and responsibilities, is often illustrated that practical lesson which society so much needs—the lesson of mutual help. It is a school where we may learn endurance and charity. Out of its trials is developed the sense of religious need; and under the shadow of its bereavements we appreciate the glorious vision of Faith. There are other issues in life, where we need these divine helps; none where we feel the need [147] of them more. Those who have stood by the sick-bed and taken the last look of the dearest earthly objects, and yet have lifted hearts of trust, and eyes of transcendent hope, are able to meet the intensest sorrows of the world, and to come out like refined gold. Home, then, should be regarded especially in this light, as a sphere where the richest elements of our moral culture are supplied.

Finally, if at home we find the most essential happiness or misery of life, of course each should do his best to make it the most *attractive* of all places. He should bring not his worst, but his best temper there. How many are there who bottle up their wrath all the day long, and uncork it when they get home! They had better reverse the process. If you must chafe under disappointment, and indulge angry passion, let it out in the excitement of the world, where the rough friction of business will help you to get rid of it, or where nobody has time to care whether you get rid of it or not.

And let *business* stay where it belongs. Do not interrupt social claims with its spe [148] culations; nor drag the counting-room into the parlor. There are some men with whom business is a disease; they are never easy with it and never rid of it. Thus, perhaps, they acquire a reputation for smartness and enterprise; but they do it, it is to be feared, by putting aside other and more sacred claims.

Nor let him who is the genial companion abroad, be the morose boarder in his own house, reserving his vivacity for society and the lees for the fireside. It is a great deal better to be like the stream that is good and welcome wherever it flows, but is sure to be fresh at its source. Indeed, there are men who are made up of foam, and sparkle, and who circulate in society, but contribute nothing to the necessaries of life, and are returned empty. It is an unfortunate gift that cheers the world outdoors, but casts only a dreary shadow inside.

Of course, in speaking of the influence of dispositions in making home attractive, I would include the duty of those who [149] stay at home as well as of those who go abroad, and that self-sacrifice and kind hearts should be found as well as brought there. Indeed, if time would allow me to make a theme of what now can be only a hint, I should dwell largely upon *woman's* influence in this matter.

But home is to be rendered attractive not only by the disposition, but by the customs of its inmates. It must be a place to live, not merely to eat and sleep in; a place where we can find entertainment, and not always leave in search of it. It is really a monstrous folly, this fashionable treatment of home, which leads people to abandon it almost every night in pursuit of pleasure, or else to sweep it with a rout, which considers a household evening very dull, and makes Sunday a day for sleeping and yawning. The central idea of home is *stability*, and this has much less chance to be realized in the city than in the country. In the latter, old forms and landmarks are not so liable to interruption, and the slow process of time works instead of the hand [150] of innovation. But in a city, where a man emigrates before he has fairly settled, and where many move with every May-day, the idea of a homestead is almost obsolete. Elegance, solidity, venerable associations, none of these can resist the march of improvement, and the rapid tide of business enterprise. The main streets of a great city in this country, may almost be termed so many dissolving views of perpetual change and renewal. But, perhaps, there is hardly one of us who does not feel that by his or her own exertions the essential element of Home can be made far more abiding than it now is; and where we hear of frivolous daughters and dissipated sons, many a parent may ask the question, "What have I done to cheer and consecrate the household world, and make it more abiding?"

My friends, when I consider the magnitude and importance of the subject now before us, and how many topics of discussion grow out of it—when I think how much must be left entirely unsaid—I entreat you not to suppose that I offer this discourse as [151] anything more than a *suggestion*—a suggestion meant to turn your attention to this subject of Home in the City, and leaving it to the elaboration of your own thoughts. Remember, here abide the deepest springs of social life. The noblest privileges, the greatest duties, find their basis here; and we are taught first "to show piety at Home." And the influence of this institution upon all other fields of human action, private or public, is too obvious to mention. All life flows from the centre, outwards; and the citizen who desires the order and purity of the community in which he lives; the philanthropist, who, under all conditions, regards the highest welfare of his race; the Christian, who urges the secret culture of the soul, must look with peculiar solicitude to this institution. It is one whose impotence is demonstrated by the strength of the instinct which creates it and clings to it—an instinct which associates the most genuine happiness with its sacred enclosure of affection, however rude or poor that spot may be—which, while a man has such a [152] place to call his own, makes him feel that he is somebody, and has some tie and claim in the world; and which, on the other hand, associated the most bitter destitution, the dreariest isolation, with that one word— "Homeless."

How this instinct abides, how long and how far it goes with us, is beautifully illustrated in the lines of Goldsmith.

> "In all my wand'rings round this world of care,
> In all my griefs—and God has giv'n my share,
> I still had hopes my latest hours to crown,
> Amidst these humble bow'rs to lay me down;
> To husband out life's taper at the close,
> And keep the flame from wasting by repose.

* * * * * * *

Around my fire an ev'ning group to draw,
And tell of all I felt, and all I saw;
And, as a hare whom hounds and horns pursue,
Pants to the place from whence at first he flew,
I still had hopes, my long vexations past,
Here to return—and die at Home at last."

Hopes, my friends, which I think glow in the breasts of most of us, and burst spontaneously from our lips. "Let us," we [153] say, "if our lot may be so ordered—if the lines of duty run not otherwise—let us live at Home." Here, amidst those darkened and brightened associations which are woven in the warp and woof of our deepest experience. Here, where gentle memories steal upon us with the shadows of the twilight, and for ever tapestry the walls. Here, where we have held delightful intercourse with man, and secret communion with God. Here, where we have tried to do our duty, and exercise our love, and to drink with patience the sweet and bitter which our Father mingles in life's mysterious cup. Here, where old friends are always cherished and new ones gladly come. Here, where the dearest ties of earth have bound us in a family circle; and though here and there we find broken links, we still keep hold of them, and they draw us up.

And when on this familiar hearth our own vital lamp burns low, and the golden bowl begins to shudder and the silver cord to untwine, let our last look be upon faces that we best love; let the gates that open into the [154] celestial City be these well-known doors—and thus may we also *die* at Home!

And this instinct of Home is not attached merely to earthly conditions, but mingles with those aspirations which flow into the illimitable future. As in the vast city we seek some enclosure of our own—some place of shelter for our heads, of sympathy for our hearts; so, respecting the destiny of the soul. In spite of all our philosophy, we cannot be satisfied with the conception of a mere immaterial essence floating hither and thither in immensity. The intellect looks eagerly forward to a boundless and excursive state; but the affections, the sentiments, yearn for some locality — some spot of residence and repose. We cannot help cherishing the conception of a place where our friends are grouped together, and whither we shall go, though to be united in wider and more glorious relations. And, knowing no better name for it, with eyes of hope and tearful rapture, we look up and call it "Home."

[155]

THE ALLIES OF THE TEMPTER.

[156]

[157]

DISCOURSE VI.

THE ALLIES OF THE TEMPTER.

He that is not with me is against me. — Matthew xii. 30.

One of the discourses of the preceding series was devoted to a consideration of the vices — especially the three prominent vices — of great cities. I propose at the present time to speak of the *Influences*, more or less direct, by which these and kindred evils are encouraged. Vice, and moral corruption of any kind, no doubt has its roots in the gross hearts and in the perverted appetites of men. But the most superficial observer must see that these are nourished not merely by their native soil, but by the social atmosphere which spreads around. Of course character constitutes the man, and, however this may be affected by circumstances, it enfolds the consciousness of an original per [158] sonality acting upon and through and in spite of its conditions. Nevertheless, the ingredients of this very personality are assimilated out of these conditions, and it is difficult to limit or define the subtile elements that blend in the deepest currents of a man's nature. It is, at least, a simple truism that he differs in one state of society from what he is in another. And, therefore, among the forces which help make up his moral condition, we must calculate the social forces. His virtues are not all self-sustained, and his vices draw nutriment from fine and remote channels. It would be an interesting process to analyze our own habits and temper and cast of thought, and find how much of this is involved with our physical relations. The air we breathe, the house in which we dwell, the very way in which it fronts the sun, the degrees of light and of shade that fall upon us with the flying hours, all weave their delicate influences into the tissues of our being. And how much that we do not suspect comes to us, day by day, in social intercourse, in the bearing of friends, in the tone and air of conversation, in the mere [159] magnetism of the parlor or the street! How much to strengthen or to weaken us; to clear or to cloud our moral atmosphere; to make us fresh and decisive, or to slowly sap our virtue! But it is a more solemn task to compute the influences that proceed *from* us, and to discover how, unknown to ourselves, we are swaying the circles of other lives. Why, the mightiest forces go silently. You do not see the gases that compose the vital air. You do not feel the aroma that steals along loaded with poison, or wafts a blessing through the sick man's window. You do not hear the electric pulse that beats in the summer light and in the drop of dew. Neither can you estimate the mysterious attraction that plays all through this network of social relations, nor the energy of good or of evil with which it is charged not merely from your words and deeds, but from the still reservoir of your example.

When I look around at the prevalent vices of the city, then, and at its various forms of corruption, I am not willing to rest with the mere assertion, that all this is the fruit of per [160] sonal sin and folly on the part of those who have yielded to temptation. It *is* the fruit of personal sin and folly. And we, perhaps, in our serene respectabilities, shrink back and wonder at it. It *is* strange — is it not? — that the young, the fair, the gifted, should yield themselves to that arch-deceit which has allured and ruined men for six thousand years? Is it not the same old guilt, the same sophistry and foolishness, here in New York, that it always has been? Did it not bear the same Circean cup through the halls of Nineveh and Babylon, and fling Cæsars and Alexanders to the ground? Did it not wear the same seductive smile and harlot tinsel when it walked the streets of Tyre, and reclined in the decorated chambers of Egypt? And will not its votaries find now, as then, that it entices with the embrace of death and the fascination of hell? Why should they thus float upon the very rim of this great whirlpool, and not notice the groans that come up from its depths; and see that its phosphoric illusion is mixed with fiery flakes of torment and the foam of despair? It is indeed wonderful that so many [161] should be thus deluded over and over again; so many noble energies thrown away, so many sanctions trampled upon, so many bright hopes quenched for ever. It is wonderful that any being made in the form of man, should cast down his prerogatives and wallow like the beast. Sufficient evidence of sin and folly in those who do this, to be sure; but in what way do these allurements present themselves? What are the resources and entrenchments of these vices, by which they act upon human appetite and passion? You point me to brilliant windows and gay apartments; to sparkling glasses, and shining heaps, and shapes of painted shame. "These," you say, "are the forms which the

Tempter assumes. Under smiling features and fair garlands, he hides at first that hideousness which in due time is revealed to his victims. From the lighted vestibules which open so easily to the touch, and where all seems only a coronation of youthful pleasure and natural joy, the feet of men slide downward into those abysses which are hidden from the public gaze, and over whose depths the blackness of darkness broods." And [162] all this, again, is true. These are the ways in which the Tempter works. But is there nothing but this to explain the power which evil has upon men, in the midst of the great city? These manifold allurements, these haunts of infamy and shambles of destruction—I see them standing upon strange foundations. I see them propped by these very influences to which I have alluded; influences of social condition and individual example. They would not be so formidable, they would not stand so long, were it not that respectability in its daily walk and conversation; and social culture in thousands of homes; and even justice in its lofty seat; lend them support. "He that is not with me is against me," said Jesus; and, taking this proverb as a rule, a good many people may be surprised to find that, in one way and another, they are *Allies* of the Tempter.

The allies of the Tempter, I propose to speak of now—not the forms of Temptation, which I have already illustrated. Nor do I intend to dwell upon those *direct* conditions of moral evil, out of which vice and [163] crime grow as spontaneously as weeds out of a damp and neglected soil—those wide seed fields of *ignorance* and abject *poverty* which lie around us. But the more remote and indirect causes it may be profitable for us to consider; and to these I now proceed.

I observe, then, in the first place, that the Tempter has one Ally in *Public Sanction*. There are sources of vice and crime that are permitted and encouraged by *Law*. I hardly need specify the prominent instance to which I allude. But I am not aware of a more enormous public inconsistency than what is termed "the License System"—the system of permitting the sale of intoxicating drinks in a degree, and of restricting them in a degree. For, by this method, either a moral wrong is committed, or else a civil one. If these drinks are an individual and public injury; if they distribute the seeds of disease, crime, death, and every form of social misery; then what right have we in any respect to set upon them the solemn sanction of a Law? If, on the other hand, they are a benefit to mankind; a good gift of Provi [164] dence, as some seem to think; why should we hamper their circulation? Why should we allow one man the privilege of distributing such a blessing, and forbid another who, no doubt, is equally zealous for the public good?

But this very system is a confession by public opinion, in its most authentic form of expression, that the sale of intoxicating drinks is an evil. "Only," we are told, "as it is a prevalent and deep-seated evil, it must be *regulated*." But how can we regulate an irregularity? How can you regulate an obstruction that is involved with the springs of a machine, or the works of a clock? The only possible method obvious to common sense, would be to remove the obstruction; and it would be thought the most foolish speculation conceivable for one to spend his ingenuity in contriving some way to keep the obstruction where it is, and yet to keep the clock going as it ought. If it moved regularly, the matter referred to would not be an obstruction; and if it did not, the contrivance to keep it there would [165] be a help to the obstruction. Now, I consider this great vice of Intemperance a decided obstruction in the clock-work of an individual man, or the more general mechanism of society. It transforms a great many faces into bad dial-plates, disturbs the pendulum of public order, makes people go much too fast, and renders them liable to strike at all times. Now, if a man, or a community, can be made to go just as well with it as without it, we certainly need no legislation, for there *is* no obstruction. On the other hand, if it is essentially an irregularity, the only rational method is to get rid of its accessories altogether. To enact some way in which the irregularity shall work, is to confirm and sanction the irregularity. And the license-system — for I wish to be plain and specific here — confirms and sanctions the agents of intemperance. It indicates a way in which the irregularity may work.

And not only is vice thus aided by the Law. The existence of such a sanction engenders either an error or a moral wrong. For it indicates that the sale of intoxicating drinks is [166] a public benefit, which is false; or, on the other hand, that it is lawful to uphold an evil. The same principle carried out by individuals, would excuse almost any fault. The man who steals a loaf of bread may contend that it is a necessary expedient; and he who fills an empty purse at his neighbor's expense, only endeavors to regulate an irregularity.

But suppose we make the system a strict one, what process should be employed? Probably you would say—"break up all these filthy and low haunts; all these places where the habitually intemperate, the degraded, the wretchedly poor congregate; and let these beverages be sold only in respectable places and to respectable people." But is this really the best plan? On the contrary, it seems quite reasonable to maintain that it is better to sell to the intemperate than to the sober—to the degraded than to the respectable—for the same reason that it is better to burn up an old hulk than to set fire to a new and splendid ship. I think it worse to put the first glass to a young man's lips, than to crown with madness an old drunkard's life-long alienation—worse to wake [167] the fierce appetite in the depths of a generous and promising nature, than to take the carrion of a man, a mere shell of imbecility, and soak it in a fresh debauch. Therefore, if I were going to say where the License should be granted in order to show its efficacy, I would say—take the worst sinks of intemperance in the city, give them the sanction of the Law, and let them run to overflowing. But shut up the gilded apartments where youth takes its first draught, and respectability just begins to falter from its level. Close the ample doors through which enters the long train of those who stumble to destruction and reel into quick graves, and let the flood overwhelm only the maimed and battered conscripts that remain. Besides, it is better to see vice as it really is, than as it sometimes appears. The danger of intemperance is when it assumes this very garb of respectability, and sits in the radiant circle of fashion attended by wit and beauty and social delight. Let us see the Tempter, not as he seems when he throws out his earliest lures, in festal garments and with roses around his brow; but as he looks when fairly engaged [168] in his work, showing his genuine expression. Let us see this vice of intemperance in its *results*, as they teem and darken here in the midst of our city life. Lay bare its channel— let us see to its very depths—where it flows over the wrecks of human happiness, and over dead men's bones. Lay bare its festering heaps of disease, its madness, its despair, its domestic desolation, its reckless sweep over all order and sanctity; and thus, tracing it from its sources under glittering chandeliers and in fonts of crystal, we shall be able to say—"this is the real element which exists and does its work, by public connivance and with the sanction of Law!"

If you ask me then, whether I think that a statute of absolute prohibition would stop this flowing curse, I reply that at least it would put the influence of authority on the right side. It would lend it the force of consistent endeavor. As it is, it would be far better if the public sanction had no expression; for now it only confirms and guarantees the evil. Its power is exerted not in the right, but in the wrong direction. It is an ally of the [169] tempter. For the spirit of everlasting Justice and Benevolence, speaking as it were by the mouth of Jesus, says—"He that is not with me is against me."

But I observe, in the second place, that the forces of temptation in the city are nourished by *public neglect*. In individual experience it will be found, I think, that sins of *omission* are more numerous and are worse than sins of *commission*. If we examine our lives closely, we shall discover that our moral indebtedness comes even less from what we have done, than from what we ought to have done. And this individual experience has a counterpart in social conditions. How many evils among us grow up under the shadow of inoperative laws—laws which have a voice and nothing else—nay, hardly a voice, so seldom are they heard even to speak. They appear to have been enacted merely as a compliment to decency, and they remain in the statute-book as "idle as painted ships upon a painted ocean." The dens of debauch keep open doors night and day; the saloons of profligacy send out their cards of invitation; the gambler rattles his [170] triumphant dice; but excursive policemen never see, and vigilant magistrates never hear! Some provision of nature has imparted a very singular quality to the optic powers of the one, and the auditory nerves of the other. The laws against this vice, or that custom, stand fixed and silent; and as for putting them in operation, one would as soon think of pulling up so many grave-stones. They *are* the grave-stones of a dead public sentiment—the stumbling-blocks of a blind justice, that too often shakes hands with the very guilt which it professes to condemn. I do not, by any means, believe that everything is to be accomplished by law. I do not believe that the profoundest results are to be accomplished by it. But, if it possesses any efficacy at all, it consists in its power to repress open and shameless wrong; and where any such wrong *is* open and shameless, public neglect is the cause, and such public neglect, therefore, is an Ally of the Tempter. And let us consider the enormity of such evils. In every great city there are some omissions of executive duty, which, though grievous to be borne, are noticed with good humor. But [171] there are moral swamps, sending up their foul steam to pollute the common light; there are kennels of uncleanness, running with the waste of human lives, sweeping along with the death-gurgle of human souls; there is a dry-rot of impurity infecting the town-air, withering the dearest sanctities of society and of home—and over this kind of evil we cannot be facetious. Think how much is risked here, and how much is lost! Domestic happiness, reputation, honor, health, order, the prospects of the young, the peace of the old—Fathers, the hopes of your sons! Mothers, the interests of your daughters! and, though speaking may have little effect, say whether we ought not to speak, and to speak indignantly, of the neglect which lets these evils spread with deadly luxuriance, and winks at them as though they were harmless?

But, my friends, what do we mean by "public sanction," or "public neglect?" There are some convenient synonyms which help us to cover up our personal responsibility—help us to transfer our own sense of duty to a vague secondary agent, and keep peace with [172] our own consciences. And yet they are only *synonyms*, after all. Now this term "public" is but another word for the aggregate of our personal obligations, and does not for a single moment rid us of our share in the general influence. The real point of my present topic is this—you and I and every other individual involved in this network of social relations, are helping or weakening the force of these prevalent evils. And it may arouse us to some decision of conduct to consider how the most respectable—those who would shrink with horror from these foul customs—are, nevertheless, Allies of the Tempter. And I might state, as a comprehensive proposition, that every man *is* an Ally of the Tempter, who does not put forth a conscious and positive moral energy; who does not habitually throw his example and his influence in the right direction. It is not enough that he abstains from wrong himself—that he is chaste, and temperate, and upright, and unimpeached. For perhaps the most hopeless people, morally speaking, are those people who, according to their own confession, "have never done any [173] harm." There is a good prospect for those who are trying to grow better, however they may slip and flounder. There is hope, on the other hand, for the desperately wicked — for the very violence of one extreme precipitates the other; and sometimes the best and purest souls have been swept by a thunder-shower of sin. But those who rest upon the fact that they "have never done any harm," by being so easily contented show but little moral vitality. There is no aspiration in their natures. They seem to have no particular mission in the universe; for, if they have never done any harm, they have done little else. They are poorly fitted for this earth, which demands the effort of all our faculties; poorly fitted for heaven, whose inhabitants would not make harmlessness their chief characteristic. Their residence and their paradise might be a great exhausted receiver, where there is no gravitation to draw them down, and no air to send them up. But, in truth, these people deceive themselves. Every man exerts a *positive* influence, and cannot, if he would, be a mere negation in the world. In the great con [174] flict of good and evil there is no middle ground. There are no compromises in God's government, and neutral men are the devil's allies. "He that is not with me, is against me."

Let us see, then, how possible it is that *we* may contribute to the force of evil in the City. In other words, let us inquire — in what way do respectable and harmless people, as they deem themselves, become Allies of the Tempter?

In the first place, by their *customs*. And, chief of all, by the custom of an intense and inconsiderate selfishness. How many there are who require no other sanction for what they do than "that pleases me," or "this gratifies me!" It is wonderful what a mighty agent *self* is, estimated by its own standards. It is the hero of every exploit, the centre of every event, and the oracle of all opinions. It interprets the purpose of the universe; it finds out exactly what the world was made for. At least, a good many, apparently, have ascertained that the world was made for them, and that they were sent into it to get what [175] gratification they can. And it appears sadly out of tune to them, if it does not serve this end. In anything they do, therefore, they consider only selfish consequences. They do not apprehend the universe in its great harmony. They do not trace out its web of mutual relations — a braid of light held in the hand of Infinite Love. They do not know the sympathy that shoots in the crystal, and shimmers in the aurora, and beats in the heart of the ocean, and makes the silent music that rolls from sphere to sphere along the glittering scale of heaven. If they did, they would discover, perhaps, that the social world is constructed upon the same plan; and man cannot be an alien from the common humanity however hard he may try. Yes: concerning any custom, you have not only yourself to consider, but the bearings of its influence throughout this tissue of hearts and minds with which you are involved. You cannot isolate yourself from your responsibilities. You cannot shut yourself within comfortable walls, and say—"Here is the limit of my obligations, and here I will do as I please!" You may *say* this, but [176] you do not rid yourself of these claims. Through imperceptible aqueducts your influence runs abroad; and what you do, and what you are, contributes particles of disease or health to the social atmosphere that envelopes all. I look around, then, upon the vices and even the crimes of the City, and I say that some of them find root in the customs of the respectable and the fashionable. Profligacy, which we shrink from in its open profession, and which appears abominable in its avowed haunts, finds encouragement wherever the libertine receives the smile of beauty, and the guilt of the meanest sort of a man is excused on account of an agreeable manner. Thus the poison of the snake, and the blight of his venom on many a reputation and many a womanly heart, is all forgotten in the drawing-room, because of the fascination of his hiss and the glitter of his skin. Again, the Tempter has an Ally in the world of Traffic, wherever bad things are stamped with respectable names—when, for instance, swindling is called "smartness," and robbery "per-centage." Among people of less note in the world these [177] matters are named "cheating" and "stealing," and some of them may take punishment the more reluctantly because they cannot perceive the difference. And, still again, I think that a little use of intoxicating drinks is like the little matter that kindles a great fire, and that there would not be so much intemperance if there were not so many "temperate" drinkers. The sluices of the grog-shop are fed from the wine-glasses in the parlor; and there is a lineal descent from the gentleman who hiccups at his elegant dinner-table to the sot who makes a bed of the gutter.

"Am I my brother's keeper?" asked the first man who reddened his hands with the violated life of a man; and the answer came crying upward in a voice of blood from the ground. "Am I my brother's keeper?" *you* ask, perhaps, with a tone of surprise or scorn. *You* ask O! respectable gentleman or lady; O! man in the thick of business; O! self-indulgent Epicurean;—and the answer comes to you not from the ground merely, but from the universal air—the answer of kindred pulses, of confluent sympathies, of an insepara [178] ble humanity—though it swarms in rags, and riots in shame, and seems far off from you in its hell of debasement and despair. Nay, perhaps the answer comes very *near* to you. It may come from some one of your own household. You may ask—"Who has tempted even my very child?" Ask *Yourself*—"Need he have gone outside this very door to find temptation?" Ah! perhaps you are not merely an Ally of the Tempter, but have furnished conscripts for his vast army. Your children perhaps will rise up and call you—*not* "blessed." And see, too, what kind of conscripts the Tempter draws from the ranks of respectable and especially of fashionable life. Mere striplings, so dwarfed and dwindled by precocious dissipation that they look like feeble specimens of wax-work; whose faculties—the evident product of a thin soil—have been developed by bottles of wine and fast horses; whose memories are too short to remember their parents; whose ideas are too artificial to touch any genuine spring of nature; who are ashamed of true manliness, and make a miserable farce of what they *call* [179] "manliness;" and who, as they parade the streets, make up a sort of bombastic interlude in the drama of "Young America."

But, whatever view we may take of this general subject, it is evident that we cannot easily exaggerate the influence of "respectable and fashionable" customs upon the forces of temptation. And, surely, it becomes each of us to consider the tendencies of his own example, and ask—"Is it toward the right or the wrong? Is it for, or against the good?"

Again, the Tempter finds help from our *indifference*. This, indeed, may be the qualification which should be applied to the remarks I have just made. It is not to be supposed that the evil influences which go out from the customs alluded to, are the results of *intention*. They spring up in a lack of interest and of the consciousness of duty. They grow rank and luxuriant in neglect. If we were only in earnest as to these vices and crimes and guilty customs; if we would only wake from our apathy, to reflection and conviction; how soon would they diminish, and how many of them would pass away!

[180]

But, as comprehensive of this, and in fact all the rest that may be said, I observe, finally, that the temptations of a great city are strong because of a lack of the spirit of *Christian love*. In one respect, especially, is it true that men in general are not *with* Jesus, and therefore are against him. They have not his sympathies, his spirit of self-sacrifice, his broad, deep, universal charity. Baneful customs, and cold indifferentism grow up in a soil that is watered by no living and unselfish love. They show the dryness and the baseness of our social state. And it is not merely in the lack of active and practical love that the Tempter grows strong; but in the exercise of a prevalent *uncharitableness*. Too many of us have no disposition but scorn for the fallen; see no blessed possibilities in them; do not detect any divine ray glimmering in the thick darkness — do not discern the precious soul, like a crown-jewel, in its filthy and battered casket. And if this paralyzes and kills the springs of our own activity, need I say how the hearts of the offending are repelled and hardened in such a hostile atmosphere? Need I say how [181] desperate is the Ishmaelitish conviction; the sense of isolation and antagonism; and, on the other hand, how powerful and healing, even for the most distant and hopeless, is the sweet attraction of sympathy? And what are we, that we dare to cherish this exclusive horror, this pitiless, unrelenting scorn? When we consider our own slips, compared with our temptations; the account to which God may hold us, not the smooth standards of human respectability; how much higher is our own moral level, that we feel no chords of a common humanity reaching down even to those fallen ones, and cannot stoop to touch them? My friends, it may be, after all, that the Tempter has no surer ally than the averted face of contempt and the word of unsoftened rebuke, driving the barb of conscious guilt deeper and despairingly into a brother's soul.

And, as I look upon this mass of social evil, these steaming wells of passion, these solid fortifications of habit where the Tempter is entrenched, I ask how is all this to pass away? And the answer is—only by the spirit of [182] Christian Love, sweeping these impediments of selfishness from the heart, and animating us to effort. *With* Christ the work certainly can be done. In this Gospel-beating amidst the guilt and sorrow of the world like the pulsations of a Divine heart—in the few leaves of this Testament—there is an illimitable power, before whose inspiration in the purposes and deeds of men no evil thing shall stand. And the spirit and exercise of this Love *is* Religion. It is the up-shot of all that is preached—it is the open and tangible test of every mystic experience that drifts through the soul—it is so deep, so broad, and runs so far, that it comprehends all requirements; and they who cherish it, and practice it in the low and dark and desolate places of the world, are the true saints. Nothing else will do in its place. Not Churches, nor creeds, nor rituals, nor respectabilities. Without it we are not friends of Christ, nor co-workers with God. Without it we deepen the channels of human woe, and prop the strong-holds of wickedness. Without it, whatever we may not be, we are Allies of [183] the Tempter. The Saviour says to each of us to-day, placed amidst these antagonistic forces of Life—"He that is not with me is against me."

[184]

[185]

THE CHILDREN OF THE POOR.

[186]

[187]

DISCOURSE VII.

THE CHILDREN OF THE POOR.

The young children ask bread, and no man breaketh it unto them. —
Lamentations iv., 4.

The writer of these words bewailed a state of War and Captivity — a state of things in which the great relations of human life are broken up and desecrated. But it is strange to find that the most flourishing forms of civilization involve conditions very similar to this. For, if any man will push beyond the circle of his daily associations, and enter the regions of the abject poor, he will see how the hostile forces of privation, and hunger, and unguided impulse, have laid waste the sanctities of existence in the abodes and in the breasts of thousands as with sword and with fire. There [188] is no essential difference in starvation, whether it ensues from the ravages of an invading host or from the lack of means. Temptation is a fierce legion; and death looks no more terrible under a Babylonian helmet, than it does upon the gaunt faces of men who die upon the bare floor or wallow in rags. The worst calamity *in* a calamity — if I may use such an expression — the most deplorable thing in any of the great evils of life, occurs when the selfish instinct within us is aroused, by want or terror, to such a degree that it overwhelms all social limitations, absorbs every sympathy, and leaves nothing but an intense individualism. This is the result in a sudden shock of danger, when the alarmed instinct is the first that starts to the summons. Sometimes, in protracted peril, it grows into an actual delirium of selfishness, and drowns even the sense of fear — as men amidst the horrors of a shipwreck will commit the most brutal excesses, and even rob the dying. And thus, in the desolation of Jerusalem as described by Jeremiah, the very yearnings of maternity were swallowed up by this fierce instinct.

[189]

> "The hands of tender-hearted women cooked their own children;
> They were their food, in the destruction of the daughter of

my people."

And results as bad as this appear in the conditions of poverty, suffering, and social degradation. Every fine chord of human nature is seared, sodden, torn from its sockets, in the darkness of the moral faculties and by the pressure of animal wants. The poor man is conscious of nothing but privation and suffering. He gazes at the power and discipline and pomp of society all about him, not as an ally but as a captive, or as a savage foe. The whole wears the aspect of a besieging army, and the Ishmaelitish feeling predominates. In the midst of the City he becomes an Arab of the desert, a robber of the rock. Now, it makes little difference whether the circle is wider or narrower, whether the siege is a moral or a literal one, whether the agent is the sword or the condition of society. The essential results will be the same. The civilization of New York may and does hem in a desolation as fearful in kind as that of Jeru [190] salem, and involves sufferings as keen, and wakes up instincts as fiercely selfish. And one whose sympathies with the wide humanity are as fresh and clear as the Prophet's were with the woes of his people, might draw closer within these various circles of prosperity and refinement and activity, that lend such attractiveness to the great city — this magnificent girdle of commerce, embossed with the symbols of all nations — these arteries of traffic, filled with circulating wealth and power — these groups of fashion and of beauty, whose cheapest jewels would open the kingdom of heaven to ten thousand souls; he might pass within all these bands of "civilization," and in some alley, or "Five Points," sit down and weep for the calamity of his brethren. He would behold there War and Captivity enough to fill an entire volume of Lamentations. Captivity! were men ever bound by a darker chain, or trampled by a harder heel, than those victims of destitution and of their own passions? War! did the Jew behold any hosts more terrible pressing into Jerusalem, than you and I might see if we looked about us? The [191] entrenched filth that all day long sends its steaming rot through lane and dwelling, through bone and marrow, and saps away the life. Cold that encamps itself in the empty fire-place, and blows through the broken door, and paralyzes the naked limbs. Hunger that takes the strong man by the throat, and kills the infant in its mother's arms. And still another traitorous legion that, equipped with the fascinations of the bottle and the shamelessness of harlotry, appeals to the passions of the brutal and proffers comfort to the hearts of the sad. War and Captivity in the midst of peace and refinement — is it not, my friends? And, with all this, may we not expect that fierce instinct of selfishness which overwhelms every other impulse, and breaks out in crime? Ah! and do we not discover a counterpart to that saddest feature of all in such circumstances — a desecration even of the parental instinct? Fathers, beating their sons into the career of guilt; and mothers — worse than those who made horrid food of their own children — offering their daughters to the Moloch of lust in the shape of some "gentlemanly" [192] devil with a portable hell in his own breast!

And it seems to me that if one with a prophet vision and a prophet heart, widened to the compass of humanity, should thus go into these waste places, nothing would affect him more; nothing would strike a deeper and tenderer chord in his bosom; than the condition of these little ones amidst the siege and terror. And, comprehending all their need — their moral as well as their physical destitution — he might exclaim, as describing the most pitiable spectacle of all — "The young children ask bread, and no man breaketh it unto them."

And I think that every one of you who has reflected at all upon this subject, must feel that, of all the conditions of Humanity in the darker regions of the City, there is none more sorrowful, more momentous, and at the same time more hopeful, than the condition of the Children of the Poor. And I do not call your attention to this subject to-night with the expectation of proclaiming any fresh doctrine, or offering any novel suggestion, but because in a series of discourses like the present I can [193] not consistently pass by such a prominent phase; and more especially because I wish to push the old truth from your heads into your hearts, so that you may be excited to immediate and practical action.

I purpose then, in regard to the Children of the Poor, to maintain one or two *principles*, to state a few *facts*, and to consider some *remedies*; and these will constitute the divisions of my discourse.

In the first place then, I lay down a general principle which divides itself into two specific principles. I maintain that we are under peculiar obligations in regard to children. Of all our duties, except those which we owe directly to God—of all the ways in which we are required to *show* our duty to God—I know of none more peremptory than this. It is the obligation of an instinct that appears everywhere; that swells in the breasts of the rudest people; that mingles with the most tender and beautiful and sacred associations of human life.

Childhood and Children! is there any heart so sheathed in worldliness, or benumbed by sorrow, or hardened in its very nature, as to [194] feel no gentle thrill responding to these terms? Surely, in some way these little ones have "touched the finer issues" of our being, and given us an unconscious benediction. Some of you are Mothers, and have acquired the holiest laws of duty, the sweetest solicitudes, the noblest inspirations, in the orbit of a child's life. And, however wide the circle of its wandering, you have held it still, by some tether of the heart, bound to the centre of a fathomless and unforgetting love. Some of you are Fathers, and in the opening promise of your sons have built fresh plans and enjoyed young hopes, and even in the decline of life have walked its morning paths anew. Many of us have felt our first great sorrow, and the breaking up of the spiritual deep within us, by the couch of a dead child. Clasping the little lifeless hand, we have comprehended, as never before, the *reality* of death, and through the gloom, covering all the world about us, have caught sudden glimpses of the immortal fields. And, all of us, I trust, are thankful that God has not created merely men and women, crimped into artificial patterns, with selfish [195] speculation in their eyes, with sadness and weariness and trouble about many things carving the wrinkles and stealing away the bloom; but pours in upon us a fresh stream of being that overflows our rigid conventionalisms with the buoyancy of nature, plays into this dusty and angular life like the jets of a fountain, like floods of sunshine, upsets our miserable dignity, meets us with a love that contains no deceit, a frankness that rebukes our quibbling compliments, nourishes the poetry of the soul, and, perpetually descending from the threshold of the Infinite, keeps open an arch-way of mystery and heaven.

And now, just consider what a child *is*—this being thus fresh from the unknown realm, tender, plastic, dependent; a bud enfolding the boundless possibilities of humanity, and growing rank, running to waste, or opening in beauty, as you turn, neglect, or support it—just consider what a child is; and he must be far gone in indifference or depravity, who does not recognize the specific duty growing out of a general obligation which is forced upon us by the intrinsic claims of that child's nature. [196] If we were appealed to by nothing else but its drooping reliance and natural wants, there would be enough to draw our attention to every phase of childhood that comes within our sphere.

But our purpose this evening calls us away from these brighter images of childhood, to consider those who are surrounded with the most savage aspects and the worst influences of the world. And, beside the absolute duty which is imposed upon us by their natural position, I observe that the Children of the Poor create an appeal to *prudential* considerations. They form a large proportion of those groups known in every city as "The *Dangerous* Classes." For they will be developed somehow. If they receive not that attention which is demanded by their position; if they are left to darkness and neglect; still, it is no mere mass of negative existence that they constitute. There is vitality there and positive strength, in those lanes and cellars, put forth for evil if not drawn towards the good. We must not confound ignorance with torpor of spirit or bluntness of understanding. One of [197] the most remarkable characteristics of vagrant children is a keen, precocious intellect. A boy of seven in the streets of a city is more developed in this respect than one of fourteen in the country—a development, of course, which is easily accounted for by the antagonisms with which the child has had to contend, and the devices which have been inspired by the sheer pressure of want. He has been pitched into the sea of events to sink or swim, and those sharpened faculties are the tentacles put forth by an effort of nature in order to secure a hold of life. And there is something very sad and very fearful in this precocity. The vagrant boy has known nothing of the stages of childhood, conducting with beautiful simplicity from one timid step to another, and gradually forming it for the realities of the world. But the neglected infant has wilted into the premature man, with his old cunning look, blending so fantastically, so mournfully, with the unformed features of youth. Knowing the world on its worst side—knowing its hostility, its knavery, its foulness, its heartless materialism—knowing it as the man does not [198] know it who has only breathed the country air, and looked upon the open face of nature. Is it not very sad, my friends, that the vagrant boy *should* know so much; and, without one hour of romance, one step of childish innocence and imagination, should have gone clear through "the world" which so many boast that they understand—the knave's world, the libertine's world, the world of the skeptical, scoffing, Ishmaelitish spirit? And yet he has so little *real* knowledge—there is such a cloud of ignorance and moral stupor resting upon his brain and heart! So much of him is merely animal, foxy, wolfish, and this sharpened intellect only a faculty, an instinct, a preternatural organ pushed out to gain subsistence with. It is a terrible anomaly, and yet, I say, it is none the less an active power, and shows us that, however neglected, the child of the abject poor is not dormant or undeveloped. In the first place, very likely, it has developed itself into a dogged atheism—a sulky unbelief. The brain of the vagrant boy is active with speculation as well as with practice—he has some theory of this life in which he lives, [199] and, as might be expected, a theory woven with the tissues of his own experience; woven with the shadows and the lurid lights of his lot. A gentleman passing one day through the streets of Edinboro', saw a boy, who lived by selling fire-wood, standing with a heavy load upon his back, looking at a number of boys amusing themselves in a play-ground. "Sometimes," says the writer, "he laughed aloud, at other times he looked sad and sorrowful. Stepping up to him I said—'Well, my boy, you seem to enjoy the fun very much; but why don't you lay down your load of sticks?'... 'I wan't thinking about the burden—I wan't thinking about the sticks, sir.' 'And may I ask what you were thinking about?' 'Oh, I was just thinking about what the good missionary said the other day. You know, sir, I don't go to church, for I have no clothes; but one of the missionaries comes every week to our stair, and holds a meeting. He was preaching to us last week, and among other things he said—"Although there are rich folks and poor folks in this world, yet we are all brothers." Now, sir, [200] just look at these lads— every one of them has fine jackets, fine caps, with warm shoes and stockings, but I have none;—So I was just thinking if those were my brothers, it doesn't look like it, sir—it doesn't look like it. See, sir, they are all flying kites, while I am flying in rags—they are running about at kick-ball and cricket; but I must climb the long, long stairs, with a heavy load, and an empty stomach, whilst my back is like to break. It doesn't look like it, sir—it doesn't look like it.'" Or, take the following instance, which I extract from the Records of one of the Benevolent Societies of our own city: "Can you read or write? said the visitor to a poor boy. Marty hung his head. I repeated the question two or three times before he answered, and the tears dropped on his hands, as he said, despairingly, and I thought defiantly—'No, sir, I can't read nor write neither. God don't want me to read, sir. Indeed, so it looks likely. Didn't He take away my father since before I can remember him? And haven't I been working all the time to fetch in something to eat, and for the fire, and for clothes? [201] I went out to pick coal when I could take a basket in my arms—and I have had no chance for school since.'" Now this is fallacious and dangerous reasoning, my friends; nevertheless, it *is* reasoning, and shows that the mind of the poor boy is not inactive as to the problems of life. And the intellect which is so acute in theory will soon drive to practice. Stimulated by that selfish instinct which, as I have shown, will under pressure absorb every other consideration, he speedily commences the career of *crime*. And have you ever looked into this matter of crime? Or do you know it only as a monstrous fact in the social mechanism, and in the records of human nature? If so, it would be well for us to consider the way in which it appears to the violator of right—the way in which things look to him who works *inside* the web of guilt. And we may be sure that it does not look to him as it does to us from the midst of respectabilities and comforts, or from a high intellectual and moral stand-point. Now I am not going to justify crime, or to indulge any sentiment upon the subject. But, really, one of the most practi [202] cal questions that can be asked is—"*Why* is this one, or that one, a criminal?" Do I say that the guilt should be imputed to the condition—that it is all owing to circumstances? No: but I *do* say that, in nine cases out of ten, crime is no proof of *special* depravity apart from *general* depravity, and that the circumstances have just so much weight as this—that put you or me in those same circumstances, in nine cases out of ten, we should be criminals too. In the same circumstances, my friends; and this involves a great deal. It involves an hereditary taint stamped in the very mould of birth; it involves physical misery; it involves intellectual and moral destitution; it involves the worst kind of social influence; it involves the pressure of all the natural appetites, rioting in this need of the body and this darkness of the soul. And it implies no suspicion of a man's moral standard—it is no insult to his self-respect—to tell him that, under similar conditions, it is extremely probable he would have been a criminal too. Reasoning in an arm-chair is very proper, and often very accurate, but the logic of starva [203] tion is too peremptory for syllogisms. There is a sort of compound made up of frost, damp, dirt and rags, which works double magic: it sometimes converts a thief into a philosopher, and sometimes a philosopher into a thief. I am not speaking, however, of the mere impulse of animal want, but of this condition where the counter-acting forces are dormant. And for this reason you and I can draw no immoral conclusion from the doctrine of circumstances. We could not be like the moral leper who infests the dark regions of the city—we could not be like the child of sin and shame who broods there—without losing our identity. In contemplating this matter, the feeling for ourselves should be simply one of humility and thankfulness. We have grown up in pure light and air, appeased with the comforts, and braced by at least the current morality of society. But, concerning those degraded ones, what some call "charity" is no more than "justice." It is no more than justice to say—all the conditions being considered—that as to a vast majority of them, crime is no proof of *special* depravity. It is the genuine [204] humanity that is there—not base metal. It came from the common mint—somewhere you will find upon it a faint scar of the Divine Image—but the coin was pitched into this bonfire of appetite and blasphemy, and it has come out a cinder. Thus, proud and happy Mother, might *your* boy have been a defaced and distorted being, kicked, cuffed, knotted with frost, blackened with bruises; a pick-pocket, a wharf-rat, a panel-thief; with his intellect sharpened to an intense and impish cunning—only knowing that it is a hard world, and he must get out of it what he can. Thus, fond Father, might *your* daughter, whom the very winds must salute with courtesy, have gone through the streets at night—a painted desolation, a reeling shame. Do you think these were made of better texture than those who blacken and fester yonder? Do you think that when these last came into the world there was no milk in mothers' breasts for them, no Divine solicitude about them, no tenderness in the heart of Christ; but that they were the refuse, whirled into existence as the great wheel of Life shaped the finer mould [205] of the respectable and the happy? I tell you that God made them complete souls, and stamped His Image upon them — but they have fallen into the dark and dreary ways; the fierce flames have hardened them; the foul air has tainted them; and their special depravity, over and above the common depravity, is the infection of circumstances. The young boy, the young girl, driven by necessity and sharpened with cunning, run into crime. They are all *educated*; for circumstances — not merely books — are education; but this is their seminary, and the alphabet is spontaneous, and the science of quick growth. And with the consequences of all this exposure and temptation we are all mixed up; and, if the claim of the child in its intrinsic position does not move us, *prudential* considerations should — the consideration of what society does suffer, and must suffer, if these conditions are not changed.

Such, then, are some of the *principles* involved with my theme. Let us in the second place pass to consider, very briefly, a few of the *facts*. Briefly, because I have no [206] time for details, and because the general state of the case is but too well known to you.

It is a fact, then, that there are among us a vast number of children in the most miserable and perilous condition. In the year 1849, the Chief of Police reported the destitution and vice among this class of vagrants as almost "incredible." In that report he says — "The offspring of always careless, generally intemperate, and oftentimes dishonest parents, they never see the inside of a school-room, and so far as our excellent system of public education is concerned, it is to them a nullity." It appears that, at that time, in 12 wards of the city, there were 2,955 of these children, of whom two-thirds were females between the ages of 8 and 16. I am informed, also, by the Chief of Police, that 100 per cent. should now be added to this estimate; not all attributable, of course, to growth in depravity, but to the increase of population, especially by immigration. I understand, moreover, that within the past year there have been ten thousand arrests, [207] and five thousand commitments of boys alone between the ages of 5 and 15.

These are naked statistics, affording you an outline of the actual state of things. Need I paint the costume and the scenery, and describe the sad and awful drama in which these children play their parts? I could not if I would. But think of that vast amount of young life running to waste, sweeping through the sewers of the social fabric, an under-current of taint and desolation! Think of them, starved, beaten, driven into crime not merely by necessity, but by the very hands of their parents! and think of them this night, cuddling in rags, shivering on straw, cradled in reeking filth, drinking in blasphemy and obscenity and cunning policies of sin, under that dark canopy that shuts out social sympathy, and hides the very Face of God. And if you have, I will not say parental hearts, but human souls, you will ask if there ought not to be some remedy, and will say that all who can should help in administering that remedy.

And *remedies* there appear to be, my [208] friends. For, while I said that there is no condition in the city more sad and momentous than that of these children of the poor, I said, likewise, that there is none more *hopeful*. The essential and comprehensive remedy of all I indicated in the close of the last discourse, and shall have occasion to dwell upon in the next. That remedy is the practical operation of Christianity—first of all in our own hearts, and then flowing out in action. I mean especially the *method* of Jesus, which consisted not of mere teaching but of *help*—which touched not only the issues of the sin-sick soul, but the weakness and want of the body. To the demoniac, to the leper, to the impotent man by the pool, he brought not abstract truths, but words of healing and works of practical deliverance. How striking is the fact that the freshest and noblest charities of this nineteenth century are only developments of the manner in which the Redeemer soothed the sorrows and vanquished the evils of the world! For those institutions which especially excite the public interest at the [209] present day, are those whose plan it is first to remove the children of the poor from those wretched and foul *conditions* upon which I have laid so much stress, and to lead them to a higher culture by extending, first, the hand of temporal relief. They aim to break up the sockets of custom, and to introduce the degraded child to fresh motives of action and fields of endeavor; to throw around him the atmosphere of a true home, and to blend intellectual, and moral, and religious training with that true charity which teaches one how to assert his own manliness, and support himself by the honest labor of his own hands. Now I do not wish to be invidious, I am glad that such a constellation of philanthropic promise has risen upon the dark places of the abject poor. I point with pleasure to what has been accomplished in the Sahara of the Five Points, and in what still remains to be done I discern a field broad enough to prevent collision and dispute — broad enough to employ the means and the generous energies of thousands. With equal pleasure I refer to that "Juvenile Asylum," [210] with its noble interposition ere the feet of the erring boy shall take the *second* step in crime, and which has recently rendered still more efficient its system of labor and relief by extending the benefit to girls. But as I wish this evening to concentrate your sympathies, I call your attention especially to the institution known as "The Children's Aid Society," the general character and the practical results of which I will briefly state. Its main object is sufficiently indicated by its name. Its machinery is simple, and acts upon the principle just laid down. It seeks first to remove the poor child from the coil of evil influences which have been thrown around him, and which have been daily strengthened by the sharpest pressure of animal necessities. It comprehends the two-fold benefit of *education* and *labor* in its system of "Industrial Schools." Of these, at the present time, in this city, there are eight, in which a multitude of children are educated, taught to work, supplied with a warm dinner daily, and with such clothing as they can learn to make. In connection with these there is one [211] shoe-shop, in which thirty or forty boys earn a livelihood. Another object of this society is to find employment for its beneficiaries out of the city, and during the past year places in the country have been found for one hundred and twenty-five, where their employers treat them as their own children.

In institutions like these, then, you perceive the indications of a remedy for the condition of these children of the poor — a system of help which gives something more than spiritual instruction on the one hand, something more than mere food and clothing on the other; which combines measures of relief and nourishment for the demands of our whole nature in the form of the ignorant and suffering child; and which, better than all, lifts him out of the humiliating condition of a mere pauper or dependent, and sets him in a channel of manly exertion, self-development, and self-support; which not only does the negative work of removing a mass of evil from society, but makes for it the positive contribution of an improved and educated humanity. I do not say that all the relief lies [212] here, that it will do all that is needed, or that nothing better will be devised. But I think the *tendency* of these institutions is the right one, and that they indicate the *way* in which this great social problem is to be solved. But it is not necessary to say that the faith which we cherish in such a system is dead without works; and that something more is needed than a few model institutions working here and there. This matter makes a practical claim upon us all, in the fact that, in one way or another, we may all help forward this method of relief—we may help it forward as active laborers in the very midst of the field, as teachers and missionaries, or contributors of our goods and money. Each knows what he can best do—what is his special, Providential *call* in the matter; but let him be assured that he *has* a call; and that this spectacle of exposed, needy, suffering childhood is not a mere spectacle for his sympathies, but a field white with a harvest that waits for his effort. Have we nothing but sympathies wherewith to answer the poor woman's prayer—a prayer that [213] echoes through so many hearts in this great city—"May the Lord spare my Archy from the bad boys, and from taking to the ways of his father!"

There is one thing which strikes me as very affecting in the condition of any child. It is when that condition is necessarily a melancholy one—when the circumstances which hem it around cast over the surface of that young life an abiding gloom. A melancholy child! What an anomaly among the harmonies of the universe; something as incongruous as a bird drooping in a cage, or a flower in a sepulchre. The musical laughter muffled and broken; the spontaneous smile transformed to a sad suspicion; and the austerities of mature life, the fearful speculation, and forecast of evil, fixed and frozen on a boy's face! And then the sorrow of a child is so *absorbing*—for he lives only in the present. In the afflictions which fall upon him, man has the aid of reason and faith—he looks beyond the present issue, he detects the significance of his calamity, and strengthened thus a brave heart can vanquish any sorrow. But, [214] as Richter beautifully says—"the little cradle, or bed-canopy of the child, is easier darkened than the starry heaven of man." Surely, then, it is a blessed thing to contribute aught that will lighten this gloom, and place the child in natural conditions.

But there is one phase of this subject which, in its appeal to us, is more eloquent than all the rest. It is where there are children who stand not merely in the intrinsic claim of their childhood; or in their touching sadness; or pushing their energies into vice and crime; but nobly struggling *against* the tide of evil — struggling to bear up in their lot — enduring and achieving for the sake of those who, young as these children are, are dependent on them. If I had time, I think I could write a "Martyrology;" not following the track of famous men, whose faces look out upon us from the brutal amphitheatre and from the fire with a halo of glory around them, and whom we behold, by the vision of faith, with their gory robes transfigured to celestial whiteness, waving palms in their hands; but tracing out incidents in the lives of some of the children here in our [215] city — not dead, but *living* martyrs! O! I think I *could* write such a Martyrology, with blood and tears, over many a gloomy threshold, on the walls of many a desolate room; and let future generations come and read it — a fearful record of human suffering — a sweet memorial of human virtue — when many of these old woes, we trust, shall have passed away for ever.

Permit me, in closing, to present two or three incidents illustrative of this heroism and sacrifice among the Children of the Poor.

Take, for instance, the account of a writer who tells us that in the street he "met a little girl, very poor, but with such a sweet sad expression," adds he, "that I involuntarily stopped and spoke to her. She answered my questions very clearly, but the heavy, sad look never left her eyes a moment. She had no father or mother. She took care of the children herself; she was only *thirteen*; she sewed on check shirts, and made a living for them." He went to see her. "It is a low, [216] damp basement her home. She lives there with the three little children, whom she supports, and the elder sick brother, who sometimes picks up a trifle. She had been washing for herself and little ones. 'She almost thought that she could take in washing now,' and the little ones with their knees to their mouths crouched up before the stove, looked as if there could not be a doubt of sister's doing anything she tried. 'Well, Annie, how do you make a living now?' 'I sew on the check shirts, sir, and the flannel shirts; I get five cents for the checks, and nine cents for the others; but just now they wont let me have the flannel, because I can't deposit two dollars.' 'It must be very hard work?' 'O! I don't mind, sir; but to-day the visitors came, and said we'd better go to the poor-house, and I said I couldn't like to leave these little ones yet; and I thought if I only had candles, I could sit up till ten or eleven, and make the shirts.' ... She had learned everything she knew at the Industrial School.... She never went to church, for she had no clothes, [217] but she could read and write.... 'It was very damp there,' she said, 'and then it was so cold nights.'"

I will, in the next place, introduce you to a garret-room, six feet by ten. The occupants are a poor mother and her son. The mother works at making shirts with collars and stitched bosoms, at six shillings and sixpence per dozen, for a man who pays half in merchandise, and who, when she is starving for bread, puts her off with calico at a *shilling* a yard that is not worth more than fourpence! But *he* is not the martyr in the case. When the visitor entered, her son George, about twelve years old, "was just coming in for dinner, pale and apparently exhausted by the effort of climbing the stairs, and sank down upon a rough plank bench near the door." He worked in a glass-factory, earning a bare subsistence. "He is a little old man at twelve," says the narrator, "the paleness of his sunken cheeks was relieved by the hectic flush; his hollow dry eye was moistened by an occasional tear; and his thin white lip quivered as he told me his simple story; how he was braving hunger and [218] death—for he cannot live long—to help his mother pay the rent and buy her bread. 'Half-past ten at night is early for him to return,' said the mother; 'sometimes it is half-past eleven and I am sitting up for him.' Sometimes, in the morning, she finds him awake, 'but he don't want to get up, and he puts his hands on his sides and says, 'Mother, it hurts me here when I breathe.' I can work, and I do work,' adds she, 'all the time—but I can't make as much as my little boy.'"

One more account. It is of a beggar-girl who "lives," as the narrative goes on to say, "in a rear building where full daylight never shines—in a cellar-room where pure dry air is never breathed. A quick gentle girl of twelve years, she speaks to the visitor as he enters—'Mother does not see you, sir, because she's blind.' The mother was an old woman of sixty-five or seventy years, with six or seven others seated around. 'But you told me you and your mother and little sister lived by yourselves.' 'Yes, sir—here it is;'" and at the end of the passage the visitor discovers a nar [219] row place, about five feet by three. The bed was rolled up in one corner, and nearly filled the room. "'But where is your stove?' 'We have none, sir. The people in the next room are very kind to mother, and let her come in there to warm—because, you know, I get half the coal.' 'But where do you cook your food?' 'We never cook any, sir; it is already cooked. I go early in the morning to get coal and chips for the fire, and I must have two baskets of coal and wood to kindle with by noon. That's mother's half. Then when the people have eaten dinner, I go round to get the bits they leave. I can get two baskets of coal every day now; but when it gets cold, and we must have a great deal, it is hard for me to find any—there's so many poor chaps to pick it. Some-times the *ladies* speak cross to me, and shut the door hard at me, and sometimes the *gentlemen* slap me in the face, and kick my basket, and then I come home, and mother says not to cry, for may be I'll do better to-morrow. Sometimes I get my basket almost full, and then put it by for to-morrow; and then, if next day we have enough, I take this [220] to a poor woman next door. Sometimes I get only a few bits in my basket for all day, and may be the next day. And then I *fast*, because, you know, mother is sick and weakly, and can't be able to fast like me.'"

These my friends, are some of the "short and simple annals of the poor." But those of whom Gray spoke rest peacefully in the "country churchyard;" their spirits are in heaven, and their history is em-balmed in his own immortal Elegy. But *these* records are of those who yet live and suffer—"Martyrs *without* the palm."

And could I summon them here to-night, and would the Master but enter as when upon earth, surely he would look upon them in tender pity; would bless them; would take in his arms those whom the world has cast aside and overlooked. Nay, perhaps he would transfigure their actuality into their possibility, and we might see "the angels in their faces," pleading with us before the Father's throne!

[221]

THE HELP OF RELIGION.

[222]

[223]

DISCOURSE VIII.

THE HELP OF RELIGION.

For here have we no continuing city, but we seek one to come. —
Hebrews xiii, 14.

There are a good many people who, apparently, are never troubled by any speculations arising out of a comprehensive view of things. They are keenly alive to all objects within their sphere; but their eyes are close to the surface, and their experience comes in shocks of sensation, and shreds of perception. They know the superficial features of the world and its conventional expressions; are conversant with its business and its pleasures; with the market, the fashions, the town-talk, the worldly fortunes of their neighbors. Sometimes, a powerful affliction startles them in this smooth routine, and for a moment they are surprised [224] to find how wide the universe is, and among what great realities we dwell. But, usually, their existence is a narrow revolving disc, bringing around the same group of incidents and the same associations, morning, noon, and night. They comprehend Life as they comprehend the expanse of yonder harbor, dotted with shifting but familiar forms, ruffled by a passing wind or bright under a summer sun, and whose tides duly rise and fall. But they little think of the oceanic vastness which it represents; and how its oscillations come from great currents that leap out of the Antarctic, and swell around tropical islands, and sweep the lines of continents, and roll in the Polar Sea.

These, therefore, are not perplexed by questions such as occur to him who, looking beyond his own worldly interests and the area of daily routine, takes into view the scope of being and the profounder phenomena of human life. For such a view will inevitably engender speculation, nor can he rest until he obtains some *theory* of existence. These very conditions of Humanity in the City, for in [225] stance — these conditions of poverty, and responsibility, and relationship, and privilege, and strife, and toil — yea, the lessons which come to us from the crowd as it flows through these streets; constitute a great problem, of which every thinking man will seek some solution.

Now, throughout this entire series of discourses — although I have not deemed it necessary in every instance to make a specific application — I have assumed that you and I were looking upon these various phases of Humanity from the Christian stand-point, and therefore I could not fitly conclude this work without indicating the Help which Religion affords concerning these problems of existence.

I observe, then, that while it may seem very simple to affirm that a *theory* does not, in any case, alter *facts*; yet there is often an advantage in laying down this proposition. For this leads us to understand precisely what a theory *may* do. It does not alter facts, but it throws them into new relations, and presents them in an entirely different light. Materialism, for instance, is a theory of Life; and [226] Christianity — in which term I include not only a system of Doctrines, but of practical forces — is also a theory of Life. Now, neither of these gets rid of the great facts of existence. Men sin and suffer and die, whether we adopt the one system or the other. But, surely, when we approach these facts from the side of Religion, they appear in very different lights, and are taken up with very different results, from their appearance and effect when interpreted by the creed of Unbelief. It would be very absurd then, because Christianity does not instantly abolish, or fully explain, all these strange and darker realities, to fall back upon the opposite ground of skepticism. This is only receding from the best solution to the worst — or, rather, to no solution at all. For I maintain that Christianity gives us not merely the best, but the *only* solution of these problems. It will be my purpose in this discourse, at least, to show what kind of help Religion *does* afford for Humanity in all these diverse conditions; and, having done this, I shall leave it to your own convictions to decide whether it is not a great and practical Help; and whether [227] there *is* any other help. I propose to illustrate the influence of Religion to this effect, first — as a *Conviction*; second, as a *Working Power*; and third, as an *Interpretation*.

I say, then, in the first place, that religion furnishes great help for man in the various issues of life, when he becomes actually convinced that its truths and sanctions are *genuine*. In other words, the conception of a moral government, of a directing Providence, and of eternal realities, vividly apprehended by the intellect, kept fresh in the heart, and assimilated to the entire spiritual nature, is a personal inspiration. It elevates the platform of a man's being, so that all things appear in true proportion. It clears his vision to detect principles, and endows him with moral courage. I do not know that I can better suggest its influence as a help here, in the conditions of the city, than by asking you to imagine what *would* be the state of things in the spheres of toil and traffic—in all the multiform relations of our humanity—if men really apprehended and believed it? *It*, I say—not some special dogma or institution, but the absolute spirit and truth [228] of Christianity. For I do not think that, generally, this *is* actually credited. I think that, with many professions of religion, and much outward respect for it, and an extensive circulation of vague conceptions about it, it is *not* commonly felt and vitalized—it is not apprehended in its blessedness and power, and absolute excellence. To the habits of the soul it does not represent and mean realities as a written contract does, or a bank-bill—something that men precipitate themselves upon, and that sways the undercurrents of their action. New York, with its Broadway and its Wall Street; with its proud buildings and its bristling masts; is a reality—but that city of which the text makes mention; that city which good men seek, and which in the Apocalypse of Faith they see; whose splendors glitter through the solemn twilight; nay, which hems them around for ever, and shines down upon them brighter than the noonday sun; to thousands, toiling, sinning, and suffering here, is *not* a reality. For, I ask you, my friends, if it *were* realized, could there be so much abject need among us; so much [229] stony-hearted selfishness; so much shuffling in trade, and corruption in politics, and meanness in intercourse, and foolish superficial living? I know, and you know, that one of the greatest evils is—not merely that men are worldly, irreligious, bound up in sad conditions and narrow conceits; but that they are so, because they do not apprehend the nature and do not feel the reality of religion. For I say once more, that a conviction of its reality must be a great help in adjusting the problems of life. And this, because it acts upon the centre of all the sin, and much of the suffering of the world. This personal application of religion stands before all other remedies for the removal of these evils. Others are attempted—others are, in a degree, successful; but none go so deep and produce results so sure. It seems to me that the position of humanity in this respect, is illustrated in the narrative of the Demoniac of Gadara. We are told that he had been bound with chains, but in his fierce madness had burst them asunder. And then, again, men had tried various expedients, but they could not tame him. But when the [230] influence of Jesus fell upon his soul, it took hold of it with sweet authority; the legion left him, and the poor, wounded, houseless man sat clothed and in his right mind. So is it with man in society; so is it with some of these social evils. The power of *law* has been invoked; and it has its legitimate sphere of operation. It checks the purposed violence. It arrests the overt act. It may consistently be summoned to purify all those channels of social action which it assumes to regulate; and, instead of patronizing the wrong, to set its face and hand against it. Thus it may prevent public harm, though it cannot stop self-injury, and remove occasions of temptation, though it cannot impart moral strength. It has no efficacy to change the assassin's heart, yet we call upon it to guard us against murder. We bid it close the den of infamy, though it does not quench guilty passion. And we may use it to stop the sale of intoxicating drinks, though it does not destroy the drunkard's appetite. And this indicates both the function and the limitation of the law. Thrown over the wild forces that rage in the human heart, [231] and that afflict community, it is like the fetters on the limbs of the demoniac. It may restrain for a time; but in some sweep of temptation it is spurned and snapped asunder. On the other hand, we have the expedients of the *reformer*. He comes with props and palliatives; soothing some cutaneous irritation, or removing some foul condition. And let us recognize the legitimacy of *his* endeavor. We must approach the human heart through the web of its external circumstances, as well as directly. Nay, often this is the only way by which we can get at it at all. And well may we rejoice over the rescue from specific vices, and commend the zeal and patience which fasten upon some colossal evil to batter and drive it from the world. But notwithstanding such noble achievement, how many have remained among the tombs, or gone back to the wilderness — demoniacs still! It is an old truth, but I say it as though it were in the conviction of a fresh fact forced upon me by these great problems that heave up in the currents of City Life; it is an unavoidable conclusion that there is only one influence that can make safe, and [232] pure, and strong in goodness, those recesses out of which issue so much social evil, and so much personal suffering. And that is the influence not of the law-giver, nor of the reformer; but of the Redeemer. It is that power which flows through the soul in a practical conviction of the reality of religion. It is the help which comes from its inspiration of divine truth and goodness in the breasts of individual men, turning them from evil, rendering them strong against temptation, and sending out from their lives fresh forces of righteousness and love.

Indeed, I believe that any man who really thinks and feels, and who has much experience of Life, will become convinced of the *necessity* of Religion. I would leave its claims not to the argument of the Moralist, or the advocacy of the Pulpit, but as they urge themselves upon us here out of the whirl, and weariness, and vicissitudes of the City. Surely, as its calm voice appeals to the sons of men, striving in this heated atmosphere; chasing phantoms that rise out of the dust; absorbed in the fickle game of fortune; borne along for a little [233] while on the top-waves of excitement, and then dying unmarked as a rain-drop that falls into the sea; surely as its voice appeals to these, saying—"Come unto me, all ye that labor and are heavy laden, and I will give you rest!" it strikes the deepest chords in thousands of hearts. I will not adopt now any professional argument to prove the great necessity of Religion as a Help in Life. But I would take my stand, in imagination, at some corner of yonder tumultuous street. How multiform the crowds that sweep by me; how diverse the faces; what a kaleidoscope of human conditions! And yet, when you attempt to classify them, how few are the actual *types* of men—how many fall into a common group; and when you try them by the profoundest standard—that of a common experience and common wants—how marvellously alike they all are! How similar in inward expression, the rich man who walks yonder, to that poor drudging son of toil, who bows his back and strains his sinews until they ache! How similar in effect the burdens which they both bear—the burden of wealth, and the [234] burden of poverty, in the fact that they *are* burdens upon the heart and the soul! And are they not both struggling with the realities of life, and moved by quenchless desires, and looking up into the same infinite mystery? Ah! my friends, I hardly think it would be the most effectual way to preach Religion in this church on Sunday, as a matter of course—but to stand out there on week-days, and strike the deepest chords throbbing unconsciously in the bosoms of those who pass me by. I would appeal to you, O disappointed, almost heart-broken man, who for years have endeavored to earn a competency to lift your head above the sheer necessities of life, but have failed in the chase, and been beaten back, and seen others who have exerted themselves not near as much, not so honorably, perhaps, rise to the very top of the stream and sail clear ahead;—or to you, O "favorite of fortune," as the world calls you, who find your palace to be only a stately sepulchre, in which all genuine feeling and simple enjoyment lies dead and wrapped in cerements of chilling etiquette—whose daughter, perhaps, has [235] mocked your fondest plans; or whose son has turned out a miserable weed of dissipation—a degenerate fopling, a rake, a fool;—or to you, O butterfly of fashion, sailing with embroidered wings in search of admiration and of pleasure; or still again, to you who have just gathered together the means of enjoyment, and ease, and everything, to make life pleasant, and lo! death has entered, and your hopes are darkened and in the dust; I appeal to you, O types of this streaming humanity, that wears so many masks, yet, carries under all a common heart; and ask you, if there is not some void that no earthly good can fill—that no finite thing can sustain and satisfy? Can you go on with the common business of the world, discharge all its obligations, control yourself in its excitements, resist its evil solicitations, bear up under its trials, and, finally, reach that period in life when you must ask—"What is all this worth?—these years of toil, these eager enterprises, this golden accumulation or unfortunate failure—what are they all worth, and what do they mean?"—can anybody well get along with all this, without Religion? [236] My friends, I say to you that, not consciously, perhaps, like the old saints who wrought and prayed and walked with upward-looking faces—but really, in the deep yearning and the secret gravitation of the soul—you *do* confess that here we have no continuing city, and you are seeking one to come. At least, it seems to me that without the Help of Religion, there is only the alternative of moral indifference—a cold, hard worldliness, or of recklessness and spiritual despair. And is not this the alternative which is exhibited in the midst of all our civilization—in the midst of this gorgeous materialism of the nineteenth century? Thousands, it is to be apprehended, do exhibit one or the other of those extremes which the poet has so well described:

"For most men in a brazen prison live,
Where, in the sun's hot eye,
With heads bent o'er their toil, they languidly
Their minds to some unmeaning task-work give,
Dreaming of naught beyond their prison wall;
And so, year after year,
Fresh products of their barren labor fall
From their tired hands, and rest
[237] Never yet comes more near.
Gloom settles slowly down over their breast,
And while they try to stem
The waves of mournful thought by which they are prest,
Death in their prison reaches them
Unfreed, having seen nothing, still unblest.

"And the rest, a few,
Escape their prison, and depart
On the wide ocean of life anew.
There the freed prisoner, where'er his heart
Listeth, will sail;
Nor does he know how there prevail
Despotic on life's sea,
Trade-winds that cross it from eternity.
Awhile he holds some false way, undebarred
By thwarting signs, and braves
The freshening wind, and blackening waves,
And then the tempest strikes him, and between
The lightning bursts is seen
Only a driving wreck,
And the pale master on his spar-strewn deck
With anguished face and flying hair,
Grasping the rudder hard,
Still bent to make some port he knows not where,
Still standing for some false impossible shore,
And sterner comes the roar
Of sea and wind, and through the deepening gloom,
Fainter and fainter wreck and helmsman loom."

[238]

But, before I quit this head of my discourse, let me say that in order to be accepted as the great Help of Life, Religion must in some way be *presented* as a reality. It must not be held forth as a mere abstraction—it must be precipitated into its concrete relations. Parting with none of its sanctity, it must be stripped of its vagueness and technicality, and be spoken in the fresh language of the time. I feel sure that amidst prevalent irreligion, nothing is so much needed as a definite statement of *what* religion is; and that men should learn to recognize its vascular connection with every department of action. It must be understood that "being religious" is not a work apart by itself, but a spirit of faith and righteousness, flowing out from the centre of a regenerated heart into all the employments and intercourse of the world. Not merely the preacher in the pulpit, and the saint on his knees, may do the work of religion, but the mechanic who smites with the hammer and drives the wheel; the artist seeking to realize his pure ideal of the beautiful; the mother in the gentle offices of home; the statesman in [239] the forlorn hope of liberty and justice; and the philosopher whose thought treads reverently among the splendid mysteries of the universe. I know that some will deem this a secularization of religion—a desecration of its holy essence by worldly alliances. But they are mistaken. It is a *consecration* of pursuits and spheres that have been cut off from all sacredness, and devoted to secondary ends. Are not the just, the useful, the beautiful, from God, as well as the good and the holy? And, therefore, is not any practice which serves these, a service of God? It is needed that men should feel that every lawful pursuit *is* sacred and not profane; that every position in life is close to the steps of the divine throne; and that the most beaten and familiar paths lie under the awful shadow of the Infinite; then they will go about their daily pursuits, and fill their common relationships, with hearts of worship and pulses of unselfish love; instead of regarding religion as an isolated peculiarity for a corner of the closet and a fraction of the week, and leaving all the rest of time and space an unconsecrated waste, [240] where lawless passions travel, and selfishness pitches its tents. O! if religion *were* thus a diffusive, practical, every-day reality, there would be a marvellous change in the aspects of life and the conditions of humanity around us. The great city, now so gross and profane, would become as a vast cathedral, through whose stony aisles would flow perpetual service; where labor would discharge its daily offices, and faith and patience keep their heavenward look, and love present its offerings. Yea, the very roll of wheels through its busy streets would be as a litany, and the sound of homeward feet the chant of its evening psalm.

But religion is not only a help in and for ourselves; it has a ministration for others—for this great mass of destitution and suffering that broods in the midst of the city. Christianity is not merely a theory of existence—it is a *working-power*. Its precepts are practical, and enjoin not merely states of mind and heart, but conditions of activity. There is an entire magazine of working-forces in that one great law—"Love thy neighbor as thyself." [241] Hear the words of an apostolical commentator upon it. "If a brother or sister be naked, and destitute of daily food," says he, "and one of you say unto them, Depart in peace, be ye warmed and filled; notwithstanding ye give them not those things which are needful to the body; what doth it profit? Even so faith, if it hath not works, is dead, being alone." And wherever Christianity has existed and been apprehended, it has produced beneficent results for humanity. It has gone over the earth like its Divine Author, with healing and with help for the woes of the race. Anybody who takes his stand at the head-waters of modern history, will see that a mighty energy was then poured into the world, whose influence is evident in the truest civilization, in the best results, of ages. In estimating the practical power of Christianity, we must look at the *positive* phase of things—we must consider what has actually been done; not merely what remains to be done. We must adopt proportionate standards, not the little measures of to-day and yesterday, in which the tides of human melioration may oscillate, and even [242] seem to flow backward and at the best to make slight headway. But take up the cycle of history that preceded the advent of Christianity, and compare it with the present period; and is there not an entirely different expression on the face of things, so far as conceptions of humanity and influences of philanthropy are concerned? Contrast "a Roman holiday," its butchery and its blood, with a modern anniversary that clasps the round world in its jubilee, and see if humanity has not been helped by religion. Or look back upon Grecian art and refinement, and tell me what oration or poem, or pantheon of marble beauty, is half as glorious as the plain brick free-school; the asylum of industry; the home for the penitent, the disabled and the poor? Ah! my friends, these are such familiar things that we may not think them the great things they really are; and in gazing upon the colossal evils that yet tower up before us, they may seem slight achievements. But they *are* great: and when I see the poor drunkard return to a renovated home — the demoniac sitting clothed and in his right mind once [243] more; when I see the dumb write, and hear the blind read, and little rescued children sing their thankful hymns; I think humanity *has* been helped a great deal since that Divine Teacher walked the earth, and took the lambs to his bosom, and made the foul leper clean, and partook with publicans and sinners, and bade the guilty go and sin no more. I think that currents of love and self-sacrifice, from that heart that was pierced for us upon the cross, have found their way through the channels of ages, through all the impediments of worldliness and selfishness, and inspired and blessed men far more than they know.

But if, turning from the positive achievement, you point to the evils that still exist — if you lift the coverings of respectability and custom from the ghastly facts that are embedded here in our so-called civilization; if you bid me mark the vice, the poverty, the crime, the oppression, the grinding monopoly, the prejudice, the gigantic materialism and practical atheism that are mixed up with it, and seem to be inseparable parts of it; then I ask you — how would it be *without* the Help [244] of Religion? What interpretation should we obtain from the dark creed of the skeptic, what inspiration from the philosophy of annihilation, and of fate? To say nothing of those forces of Love and self-sacrifice which it sheds abroad in the world, and to which I have just alluded, — Religion, in one single proposition, sends pregnant elements of direction and relief into the midst of these giant evils. That one proposition is the immortality of man — the priceless spirituality of every man — the ascription of a nature more glorious and imperishable than a star. Here is the spring of its perpetual antagonism to the world, and to the evil of the world. The latter bases its estimate of man upon outward conditions; estimates his name and his title, his equipage and his parentage, the bulk of his gold, the color of his skin, his *apparent* success or defeat. Christianity points to that vivid centre of a soul, in whose light all these external distinctions fade, are fused into dross, become comparatively naught. All the evil of the world stands upon the assumption of the former rule—upon the ground of external [245] and material valuation—which, as has been well observed by another, is a "method of studying the problems of the universe by fetching rules from the *wider* sphere (therefore the *lower*) to import into the *higher*.... So long as this logical strategy is allowed, the Titans will always conquer the gods; the ground-forces of the lowest nature will propagate themselves, pulse after pulse, from the abysses to the skies, and *right* will exist only on sufferance from *might*." On the other hand, I say, Religion, Christianity, starts from the centre outward—starts with the dignity and sanctity of the human soul—and in this is the great element of all progress and reform. Out of this have sprung the achievements of modern freedom. Assuming this inward birthright of every man, men have snapped feudal fetters, and broken the seals of ancient proscription, and torn up branching genealogies, and trodden diadems in the dust. It was this fact that inspired Sidney's speech, and Hampden's effort, and Washington's calm determination. It is this that erects itself against majorities, policies, institutions, chart [246] ers, and will not be beaten down, and will agitate, and will triumph. It is this that sends philanthropy upon its mission; and bids it stoop to the most fallen, and search under the darkest depravity. "Go abroad," it says, "amidst the guilt and misery of the great city. In the rags, the filth, the abomination, there are jewels fallen from heaven. There are souls upon which angels look with solicitude. There are interests for which Christ died. Search patiently, and deeply, and never give up the endeavor to find, to lift up, to restore." Is not all the spring of benevolent effort, then, in this single proposition of Religion? This one great Truth it utters amidst the suffering and injustice of the world—that men are heirs of one inheritance; possessors of a birthright by virtue of which all outward inequalities fade away. It bases a demand for mutual help and love, upon the fact that we are all on a pilgrimage—high, low, honored, degraded, master, slave, we go forth together, and these earthly distinctions all drop away. Rich man with rows of real-estate, with money safe in bank, with solid securities walled [247] around you—you will carry no more away than Lazarus yonder—in God's eyes you are no richer than he. Because here we have no continuing city. The destinies of our common humanity flow forward into another and more enduring one.

And, if still this problem of human degradation and suffering presses upon us, I say further, that where the constituents of this problem are most prominent, there religion is the most active. The heaviest poverty is belted about by the brightest charities; the hot-beds of crime generate the most radical efforts for its prevention and its cure; and while oppression is at work, setting its dark types upon virgin soil to print off its own shame and condemnation, indignant voices expose it and indignant hearts react against it. And more and more, every day, it is felt and proclaimed that religion is a working-principle — a practical power. Never was it more profoundly felt than in this very age that men must be confessors of Christianity as well as professors. And in the light of this conception, proffering fresh and willing help, Reli [248] gion walks abroad; and lo! waste places grow verdant, and the strongholds of guilt and misery sink down, and blessed institutions rise up, and industry takes the place of crime, and cursings are exchanged for songs, and the poorest sees the immortal light, and is lifted up by the grand thought — that "here have we no continuing city, but we seek one to come."

We have thus seen that Religion is a Help as to the fact of sin, when men are convinced of it as a great reality; and a help as to the fact of human suffering, because it is a working-power. But, over and above all this, there are problems that perplex us, and demand some answer; problems as to the How, and the Wherefore, and the End. There are times when our thoughts rise above all specific instances, and we take up humanity and existence as a whole, and ask — "What means it all?" Sometimes this question starts out of an individual experience. The shock of affliction has jarred our hearts; our expectations have come to naught; bereavement has broken up the routine of our life; or our own souls have [249] surprised us with sudden revelations. At any rate, we find our being here involved with mystery. There is something that our understanding cannot entirely grasp; something that our unassisted eyes cannot see. And the only help for us in such a case is the Help of Religion, presenting us, through faith, with an *interpretation* of human life — an interpretation which tells us that what we now experience and behold is

only transitional, preliminary, and that we see through a glass darkly, and it doth not yet appear what we shall be.

And is it necessary for me to dwell upon the strength which has
thus been imparted to sad and wounded spirits, when with perfect
trust in Infinite Goodness they have thus realized that they stand
only on one round of an upward course — only in a little segment of
the immense plan? I will merely say now, that if, through faith,
religion is a help to these by interpreting life in harmony with individual experience, so through this faith does it help the meditative
man troubled by the general problem of existence and humanity.
The meaning of these various conditions in the [250] city — the
meaning of these sins, and sorrows, and inequalities — the meaning
of this tide of life itself that rolls in endless succession through these
stony arteries — does it perplex you? Accept, then, the help which
religion gives by interpreting it as only preliminary and transitional;
only a portion of a wider scheme.

We commenced this series of discourses by standing, as it were,
in the street, on a level with all these phases of humanity. Ascend
now some lofty post of observation; some high watch-tower. The
mottled tide flows and dashes far below you. The sounds of strife
and endeavor rise faintly to your ears, and are drowned in the up-
per air. So in the altitude and comprehensiveness of faith, all this
that seemed so huge and startling dwindles to a little stream in the
great ocean of existence, and all these tumults are swallowed up in
the currents of silent but beneficent design. But, in the meantime,
the daylight has gone, the night-shadow has fallen, this stream of
human life has ebbed away, and all these sounds are still. See, now,
how much of your [251] perplexity came from a deceit of eye-
sight — see how the light of this world blinded you to the immensity
and the meaning of existence! See! over your head spreads the great
firmament. There are Sirius, and Orion, and the glittering Pleiades.
How harmoniously they are related; how calmly they roll! And
now, O man! fresh from the reeking dust, and the cry of pained
hearts, and the shadows of the grave, do not the scales of unbelief
drop from your eyes, when you see the width of God's universe,
and feel that His purpose girdles this little planet and steers its
freight of souls? You were deceived by your standards of greatness
and duration. You thought that this material city, with what it con-

tains, was everything. But *they* have cherished the true view, who in the spirit of the text have interpreted these Conditions of Humanity—the conditions of those who seek and sin and suffer in the busy crowd; of those who rest beneath yonder gleaming tomb-stones. And, as we read what all wise and good men have virtually said, our mortal term contracts, our immortal career opens, our years seem as ticks [252] of a clock, and the entire sum of our life but a minute-mark on the dial of eternity; and this huge metropolis becomes a dim veil, a perishable symbol of real and enduring things.

THE END.